EXAM REVISION

A2 Law
Criminal Law

Emma Bradbury
Caroline Rowlands

Philip Allan Updates
Market Place
Deddington
Oxfordshire
OX15 0SE

Orders

Bookpoint Ltd, 130 Milton Park, Abingdon, Oxfordshire, OX14 4SB
tel: 01235 827720
fax: 01235 400454
e-mail: uk.orders@bookpoint.co.uk
Lines are open 9.00 a.m.–5.00 p.m., Monday to Saturday, with a 24-hour message answering service. You can also order through the Philip Allan Updates website: www.philipallan.co.uk

ISBN-13: 978-1-84489-506-9
ISBN-10: 1-84489-506-8

Cover illustration by John Spencer
Printed in Spain

Philip Allan Updates' policy is to use papers that are natural, renewable and recyclable products and made from wood grown in sustainable forests. The logging and manufacturing processes are expected to conform to the environmental regulations of the country of origin.

P00782

Contents

Introduction

The authors

Emma Bradbury and **Caroline Rowlands** are teachers at Aquinas College in Stockport, Cheshire. They have experience of teaching GCSE Law, AQA and OCR AS and A2 Law, and law access courses. Emma has an LLB (Hons) and a Masters degree in Law and Medicine. Caroline has completed a BA (Hons), the Common Professional Examination and the Bar Vocational Course.

About this book

This book has been written to help AQA and OCR law students prepare for their A2 examinations. The topics included cover both specifications, but make sure you know which exam board you are following and get a copy of the specification if you are unsure. Your teacher may have provided you with a specification at the beginning of the course, and they can be found on the exam boards' websites.

Structure

There are 18 topics, which are split into headings marked alphabetically. Each heading is then split into numbered sections and subsections. This structure is designed to help you revise an area of law in small sections, and yet still be able to see how it fits into the topic as a whole.

Topic summaries

At the end of each topic there is a summary. The summary is a good way to remind yourself of the main points of each topic, but remember that details get you the best marks in an exam.

Tips

Tips are included in the margin. These include definitions, exam advice and extra information to aid your understanding.

Cases

You will already have learnt about a vast number of cases in class. However, it is neither necessary nor feasible for you to remember them all. We have included the best-known cases, as well as some recent ones. If your teacher has given you a different case to use as an example, then use whichever case you understand and can remember best. Examiners do not want you to memorise a list of cases. It is much better to know a few cases with some detail than a lot of cases with no detail. Cases can be used to explain a point that you are making in the exam.

Preparing for exams

Exam preparation should not take place in the couple of weeks before the exam. Checking your notes are correct, organising your file and writing revision notes can all be done well in advance and are best done throughout the course. Once you finish a module, or even one topic in a module, there is no reason not to make exam preparations while the information is fresh in your mind. There is a big difference between preparing for exams and the actual revision that you do to memorise the information. The more preparation you do in advance, the more time you will have to revise thoroughly in the weeks leading up to the exam.

Up-to-date notes

It is always a good idea to check that your notes are accurate and up to date. You might have misheard something in a lesson or written something down that is incorrect. It is essential that your notes are accurate and that you understand them. The best way to check this is to read a textbook. You may have one that you use for the course, or else you can borrow one from the library. It is sometimes helpful to read other textbooks, as they give you different explanations that you may understand better. If you are absent from a lesson, it is up to you to make sure that you copy up and understand what you have missed. Don't put it off until you are on study leave, when it will be too late to discover that you have gaps in your notes or you do not understand something.

Organising your file

The organisation of your file should be an ongoing process. By spending a few minutes on it every week, you can make sure that your notes are in the correct order and that you are only carrying around what you need for each lesson. One approach is to take the notes for each topic out of the file as you complete it. Either put them in a separate file at home (one for each module), or hold each topic together with a treasury tag. Make a title page for each topic, including which module it is from and a list of its contents.

Reading textbooks and articles

Reading is important in the study of law. When you finish a topic in class, read the corresponding chapter in your textbook to improve your understanding. You can also read chapters in advance if you know what topic you are about to tackle in your lessons. If you discover an important quote or example, write it down and put it with your notes.

There are some excellent law journals available. Find out if your library subscribes to any of them, and, if not, subscribe yourself. They include regular updates of new cases and changes in the law.

If your teacher gives you newspaper articles, information from the internet or reports from law journals, make sure that you make a short summary of the important points and add these to your notes. It is extremely difficult to revise from a textbook or a long article, so you need to pick out the significant parts.

Understanding

If you do not understand something that you study in class or read in a textbook, it is vital that you ask someone for help. This could mean asking one of your classmates to explain it to you in their own words or seeing your teacher after class. It is difficult to learn something and write about it in an exam if you do not really understand it. It will be obvious to an examiner that, you have simply memorised information. Do not wait until just before the exam to ask for help; do it while the topic is still fresh in your mind. Above all, take responsibility for your own learning.

Making revision notes

Revision notes can be made well in advance. It is difficult to revise from lengthy notes, so you need to make concise points that trigger your memory. Use your full class notes and textbooks to learn the law and then use short revision notes to remind you of the main points.

Revision notes should be clear and not simply a copy of your classnotes. Try to keep to one piece of A4 paper per topic. This may mean writing small. Use different coloured pens and a clear format, e.g. cases written in red pen, statutes written in green pen. This will make the notes stand out. Writing things down is a good way to memorise information — it is much better than simply reading it.

Your revision notes should be concise. Use abbreviations and only write down the minimum amount of information necessary to trigger your memory. For example, if you are making revision notes on *actus reus* and *mens rea*, use AR and MR. However, remember that it may not be appropriate to abbreviate terms in an examination.

Revision notes can take many forms. They can be written as a spider diagram, a table, a flow diagram or whichever way you find easiest to learn.

Planning for exams

Timetable

It is essential to organise your time in the run-up to the exams:

- You need to decide how much time to allocate to revising each topic. This will help you work out when you should start your revision programme. If you are taking exams in June, the Easter holidays are the best time to start.
- You should allocate yourself time each day for revising.
- Make a timetable that includes time for study as well as other activities that you do.
- Stick to the timetable. If something comes up, you need to reallocate the revision you were going to do to another time.
- Keep the sessions short, e.g. 45 minutes, and take breaks. Alternate the subjects you are revising within a day so you do not get bogged down with too much law.
- If you want to give yourself the best chance in the exams, make sure that you allocate ample time to revision.

The exam

Make sure you find out the exact dates and times of the exams you are taking. It may be that you are taking two or even three exams one after the other. Always double-check whether exams are in the morning or afternoon. Try to find out in advance which room the exam is going to be held in.

It is important that you know the format of the exam. Look at past papers so that you know how many questions to answer and how much time to allocate to each question.

Revision

Past papers

Looking at past exam papers is an excellent way to prepare for the sorts of questions you will face in the exam. The exam papers offer you a choice of question. Make sure that you would have been able to answer the appropriate number of questions on each past paper. There may be topics in a module that you would prefer to answer in an exam, but it is extremely risky to try to 'question-spot'. Make sure you could answer questions on topics other than your favourites, in case your favourites are not there.

Your teacher should be able to provide you with past papers but you can also get them from the exam board websites. It is useful too to look at the mark schemes and examiner's reports (available on the internet). The mark scheme lists the potential content that the examiner is expecting for each question on the exam paper. You can compare what you think you would write for a question with what the examiner is expecting to see. The examiner's report is written by the chief examiner and contains his/her overall view of the exam. He/she will remark on where candidates had weaknesses and which questions were answered well.

Techniques

There are many methods of revising and you may already know what works best for you. However, it can be worth trying other techniques. Using different coloured pens and diagrams are discussed above. You may wish to use coloured highlighters in this book to mark the important points.

When it comes to remembering cases, you can either keep testing yourself until the information reaches your long-term memory or you can try other techniques. Perhaps you could associate the name of the case and what happened with a picture. This could even be a scene. A silly image is often easiest to remember. For example, the manslaughter case of *R* v *Mitchell* involved a man having a fight in a post office with an old man, which resulted in the death of an old lady. Using characters from *EastEnders*, try to imagine Phil Mitchell hitting Jim who falls on Dot.

Another excellent way of remembering the order of something is to take the first letter of each point and make up a mnemonic. This is regularly used when learning trigonometry at school.

Some students learn best by reading out loud or hearing their notes spoken. This is called auditory learning. If you like this kind of learning, then read from your notes or revise with one of your classmates and explain different points to each other. You could even tape your voice and listen to it on your way to the exam.

Testing yourself

To commit information to memory, it is necessary to keep testing yourself. The repetition helps you learn facts and figures. There are a number of ways to do this. Getting someone to test you is always a good idea, but try to do this with one of your classmates, as asking a parent to test you can often lead to arguments.

An excellent way to test yourself is by reading through your revision notes and then trying to write down the main points. You may only remember a few the first time you do it, but with practice you will remember more and more. The more you test yourself, the more you will remember.

Timed questions

Many students run out of time in the exam, so you need to be aware of how long you can spend on each question. Practise exam technique by writing timed answers to past papers. Another useful exercise is to put your notes away and try to write down as much as you can remember about a topic in 10 minutes. Then look back at your notes to see what you have missed. The more you do this, the more you will remember each time.

The night before

Many people say that you should not revise the night before an exam. We agree that you should not still be writing revision notes, but you can always test yourself and read through your notes.

Double-check the time of the exam and prepare the equipment you will need. Your pencil case must be see-through; if you have not got one, just take your pens loose or put them in a transparent plastic bag. Your answers should be written in blue or black ink (e.g. biro), so take a few pens in case one runs out.

Exam techniques

In the exam room

Remember that mobile phones must be switched off and must not be in your pocket or anywhere near your desk. If you have a phone with you, give it to the invigilator to look after.

Get to the exam room early so that you can find your seat number and get settled. Read the instructions on the exam paper carefully.

Plan your answers

Before you start to answer the questions, read through the whole paper. It is worth writing a quick plan of your answer so that you structure it well and do not forget to include important information. There is no need to cross out a plan, as the examiner may like to see it.

Timing

You must be strict with yourself about how long you spend on each question. Find out in advance how much time you should allocate to a question worth a certain number of marks. For example, if you have to answer three 20-mark questions in 1 hour, you have 20 minutes to answer each.

Your own opinion

Most questions do not require you to give your own opinion, so it is best avoided. Starting sentences with 'I think...' is not appropriate. It is likely that a judge or legal academic has already had the thought before you, so it would be best to quote them instead. If you do not know who made a certain point, then start your sentence in a more general manner, e.g. 'It has also been remarked...' or 'Some may argue...'

In a problem question, it is not necessary to state what crime has definitely been committed. Instead, explain the more likely crime and remark that the final decision would be up to the jury.

Answer the question

This may seem obvious, but examiners constantly complain about candidates not answering the question. Students see a question on the exam paper and try to write everything they know in the hope that some of it will be appropriate. This is not what the examiners want. Make sure you read the question carefully and underline the important parts. An example of an exam question could be:

Discuss the current law on murder.

The word 'discuss' indicates that this question requires an explanation of the current law and a balanced evaluation. This means that you should include both the advantages and disadvantages of the current law. Always try to use cases to illustrate your point and include the suggestions for reform that have been made by the Law Commission and legal academics.

By making reference throughout your answer to the words used in the question, you are showing the examiner that you are answering the question set and not the one you hoped would come up.

Use examples

Students who do well in law exams include examples in their answers. This could be an Act of Parliament that created a law, a statistic, a quotation by a judge, a criticism made by the Law Commission or legal academic, or a case that illustrates a point of law. Always try to use examples in your answers, but do not just list cases. It is usually necessary to give a bit of detail about the facts of a case, or the law that it established, in order to illustrate a point.

Write in continuous prose

Answers to exam questions should be written as an essay with a proper structure and a conclusion. This is difficult in the time constraints of the exam, but you should try to avoid lists, bullet points and diagrams. Short-answer questions should always be answered in full sentences.

Good luck!

TOPIC 1 Basic elements of crime

All crimes, with the exception of those identified as 'strict liability', require the perpetrator to commit a criminal act (*actus reus*) while having the required criminal intention (*mens rea*). This requirement is designed to ensure that only those who are blameworthy of a crime are convicted and punished. The *actus reus* and *mens rea* differ according to the nature of the offence, but the prosecution must prove both components beyond reasonable doubt in order to secure a guilty verdict.

A *Actus reus*

When answering problem questions, always start by identifying the *actus reus*, then the *mens rea* followed by any defences.

The literal translation of the Latin '*actus reus*' as 'guilty act' provides a definition that is too simplistic. The *actus reus* is made up of all of the parts of the crime except the defendant's mental state. Each separate crime has its own specific *actus reus*.

While most crimes require the accused to commit a certain act, this is not always the case, and criminal liability can also arise through a failure to act (an omission) and from a certain type of conduct. Sometimes an act becomes a crime because of the circumstances surrounding it.

1 *Conduct crimes*

In conduct crimes, the *actus reus* is simply the prohibited conduct. Perjury is an example of a conduct crime, where the defendant is guilty if he or she lies under oath in court. The defendant is guilty even if the lie has no effect on the outcome of the case, for example if the judge or jury does not believe him or her.

2 *Omissions as* actus reus

An omission is a failure to do something. On the whole, English law requires a positive act. There is no provision for a 'Good Samaritan' law, so it is generally not possible to impose liability for a failure to act. An example of this is someone watching an unknown child drowning in a river and failing to assist, even though the bystander could easily save the child. In this case, there would be no prosecution, as the defendant had no legal obligation to act — there is no legally enforceable requirement for people to help each other.

However, due to the presence of duty situations in English law, occasionally the courts may find that a defendant is liable for a failure to act. In certain defined circumstances, the court may find that a person was under a *duty* to act, for example if the person in the example above had pushed the child into the river or if the child had belonged to them. In such cases, the defendant's failure to assist would probably lead to a prosecution.

Learn each situation in which a person may be liable for an omission and the corresponding case.

There are several different circumstances that will give rise to a duty to act. These are detailed below.

2.1 Duty arising from specific relationships

A clear example of a relationship that gives rise to a duty to act is that between parents and their children. Parents have a duty to look after their children and may be prosecuted if they fail to do so. This does not only include biological parents; the courts can also impose a duty even if the parties involved are not blood relations.

R v ***Gibbins and Proctor*** **(1918)**
A man and his common-law wife were living together with the man's 7-year-old daughter. They failed to feed the child and the Court of Appeal upheld their conviction for murder when she starved to death.

2.2 Duty arising from a contract

If a defendant is under a contractual obligation to act and fails to do so, he or she may be liable if the lives of others are likely to be endangered as a result.

R v ***Pittwood*** **(1902)**
The defendant was a gatekeeper at a level crossing. One day, he left the gate open and went for lunch. A hay-cart attempting to cross the line was hit by a train, and the driver was killed. The defendant was convicted of manslaughter. His conviction was based on his failure to perform his contractual duty, i.e. to shut the gate when the train was approaching.

2.3 Duty through public office

R v ***Dytham*** **(1979)**
A uniformed police officer watched a man being kicked to death but failed either to intervene or to summon assistance. He was guilty of misconduct in a public office, as he had neglected to protect the victim or apprehend the attackers. He was convicted of wilfully and without reasonable excuse neglecting to perform a duty.

2.4 Voluntary assumption of a duty

A duty to act may also be imposed where a person voluntarily accepts responsibility for another.

R v ***Stone and Dobinson*** **(1977)**
The defendants were common-law husband and wife, and both were of low intelligence. After a visit from Stone's anorexic sister, they decided to take her in and look after her. Over the following weeks she became increasingly ill. She was confined to bed and eventually died of blood poisoning as a result of infected bedsores. The defendants were convicted of manslaughter and their convictions were upheld on appeal. They had voluntarily assumed a duty to look after Stone's sister, knowing that she was relying on them, and their failure to summon medical assistance contributed to her death.

2.5 Duty arising from dangerous prior conduct

If someone creates a situation that causes risk to another's life or property, that person is then under a duty to act in order to stop, or at least limit, the harm caused. If the person does not do so, he or she may be liable for any resulting consequences.

***R* v *Miller* (1983)**
The defendant was a squatter in a house. One night, he fell asleep on a mattress while smoking a cigarette. He awoke to find that his cigarette had set fire to the mattress. However, he did not extinguish the flames but simply got up, moved to another room and went back to sleep, doing nothing to stop the spread of the fire. Significant damage was caused to the house and the defendant was convicted of criminal damage. The House of Lords upheld his conviction and said that on realising that he had created the dangerous situation, the defendant had a responsibility to limit the harmful effects of the fire. He could easily have done this by calling the fire brigade and his failure to do so left him liable for the damage.

3 State of affairs crimes

Ordinarily, the prosecution must prove that the accused voluntarily brought about the *actus reus* of the crime, i.e. the act or omission must have occurred because of a conscious exercise of will by the defendant. So, for example, a person hitting out due to a reflex action would not be liable, as the courts would be unlikely to find that his or her actions were undertaken voluntarily.

For state of affairs offences, however, the *actus reus* involves 'being' rather than 'doing' — it is the circumstances that create the offence. Thus, the prosecution only needs to prove the existence of those circumstances. Rape is an example, as it is not the sexual act itself that makes it a crime, rather the surrounding circumstances, i.e. that it was carried out without consent.

***Leicester* v *Pearson* (1952)**
A driver did not stop for a pedestrian on a zebra crossing but his actions were held to be involuntary. Another driver had driven into him from behind and pushed him forward onto the crossing.

***R* v *Larsonneur* (1933)**
The defendant was a French woman who was deported from Ireland and forcibly taken to the UK. When she arrived in England, she was promptly arrested for being an illegal alien, contrary to the **Aliens Order 1920**. She had been found in the UK when she did not have permission to be there. She was convicted and appealed on the basis that immigration officers had taken her to the UK against her will, but the Court of Appeal upheld her conviction.

Remember to include cases to improve your marks.

***Winzar* v *Chief Constable of Kent* (1983)**
The defendant was convicted of being found drunk on a highway in contravention of the **Licensing Act 1872**. He appealed on the basis that he had been taken onto the road by the police who had removed him from a hospital following complaints about his drunken behaviour. His conviction was upheld — what mattered was that he was drunk on a highway, despite the fact that he had been taken there involuntarily.

4 Result crimes

The prosecution must prove that the defendant's actions caused the prohibited result. For example, in murder cases, the prosecution must prove that it was the defendant's actions that caused the death of the victim. In order to establish this, it must prove a causal link between the action and the consequence.

4.1 Factual causation

First, the prosecution must prove factual causation — did the defendant's actions cause the harm as a matter of fact? The test for factual causation is the 'but for' test: but for the defendant's criminal action or omission, would the victim have suffered harm? If the answer is no, then the defendant is criminally liable. If something else is the cause of the damage, the defendant is not liable, as in the case of *R* v *White*.

***R* v *White* (1910)**

The defendant decided to kill his mother in order to benefit from his inheritance prematurely. He put poison in her drink, but before she consumed enough to kill her she died of a heart attack. The prosecution could not prove that the defendant's actions were the factual cause of her death — 'but for' his actions she would still have died. Nonetheless, the defendant was still liable for attempted murder.

4.2 Legal causation

Once the prosecution has proved factual causation, it must then prove legal causation. The test for this is whether the defendant's conduct made a 'significant contribution' to the result. The defendant's actions do not need to be the only or even the main cause of the harm.

This is sometimes known as the *de minimis* rule, whereby the defendant's actions have to be more than the minimal cause of the result.

Sometimes, there may be more than one factor contributing to the final result. This is described as a 'chain of causation'. For the defendant to be guilty, there must be an unbroken chain of causation directly from his or her actions to the end result. The chain of causation may be affected by a number of factors, such as the actions of the victim, the actions of a third party and the 'thin-skull' test.

4.2a Actions of the victim

The actions of the victim may break the chain of causation, but only if they are unreasonable.

***R* v *Roberts* (1978)**

The defendant was giving a lift to the victim and began touching her clothes. The victim jumped from the moving car to escape, as she thought that the defendant was going to rape her. The defendant was held liable for her injuries, as they were a reasonably foreseeable result of his actions. Only if the victim does something so 'daft' that it cannot be expected will the chain of causation be broken.

4.2b Actions of a third party

The actions of a third party may break the chain of causation, but as with actions of the victim, they will not if they are reasonably foreseeable.

***R* v *Pagett* (1983)**

The defendant was being chased by armed police. In order to resist lawful arrest, he took his girlfriend hostage. He then fired at police, using her as a human shield. The police returned fire and the girl was killed. Pagett tried to argue that he was not the cause of her death, but the court held that it was reasonably foreseeable that the police would return fire if shot at and his conviction was upheld.

If the victim has received negligent medical treatment, this will not break the chain of causation unless it is 'palpably wrong'.

***R* v *Jordan* (1956)**
The defendant stabbed the victim. The victim had been recovering well until being given a large quantity of drugs to which he was allergic. The victim died 8 days later, by which time the stab wound had mainly healed. The hospital treatment was described as 'palpably wrong' and the Court of Appeal said that as such it broke the chain of causation. This meant that Jordan was not responsible for the death. Since then, a number of cases have referred to *Jordan* as being dependent upon its exact facts, and it is unlikely to be followed. Indeed, it is rare that medical treatment would break the chain of causation, since the courts take the view that it would not have been required were it not for the conduct of the defendant.

***R* v *Smith* (1959)**
The defendant was involved in a fight with a fellow soldier, during which he stabbed the victim twice. The victim was dropped twice while being taken to the medical centre, and the medical officer failed to appreciate the severity of his injuries. After a delay, treatment was administered but it did not help and indeed may have made the situation worse. The victim died of the stab wounds and the Court of Appeal upheld the defendant's conviction despite the negligent treatment, because the stab wound was the operating and substantial cause of death.

***R* v *Cheshire* (1991)**
The defendant shot the victim after a fight in a chip shop. In hospital, the victim received negligent treatment and died a few days later after developing a respiratory infection causing breathing difficulties. The defendant's conviction for murder was upheld, despite the fact that the original wounds were no longer life-threatening when the victim died. The Court of Appeal held that even if the negligent treatment is the immediate cause of death, it will not break the chain of causation unless it is so independent of the defendant's actions that it renders them insignificant.

Switching off a life-support machine will not break the chain of causation.

***R* v *Malcherek and Steel* (1981)**
Malcherek stabbed his wife, who subsequently suffered irreparable brain damage from a blood clot. Steel attacked his victim with a large stone, causing severe head injuries. Doctors carried out the relevant tests on both victims and then switched off their life-support machines when it was determined that they had suffered brain death. Both men were convicted of murder and appealed on the basis that the cause of death was the switching off of the life-support machine. As doctors will not switch off machines until tests have established brain-stem death, the Court of Appeal upheld both murder convictions.

The rule is sometimes referred to as 'you take your victims as you find them'.

4.2c The 'thin-skull' test

If some pre-existing weakness or medical condition of the victim makes the result of an attack more severe than it would be ordinarily, the defendant cannot argue that the chain of causation has been broken.

***R* v *Blaue* (1975)**
The defendant stabbed his victim after she refused to have sex with him. In hospital, the victim refused a blood transfusion on the grounds that she was a

Make a case list to help with your revision. Write down the name of the case, brief facts and the point that it is used to illustrate.

Jehovah's Witness and it was against her religious beliefs to undergo the procedure. Medical opinion was that she would not have died if she had had the transfusion. The defendant's conviction for manslaughter was upheld, despite his argument that the victim's refusal to accept treatment was unreasonable and should therefore break the chain of causation. The court took the view that the defendant had to take his victim as he found her, including any religious beliefs that she may have held.

B *Mens rea*

Mens rea is Latin for 'guilty mind' and concerns the criminal intention of the defendant when the *actus reus* is committed. Along with the *actus reus*, it is a necessary requirement of all criminal offences, except those classed as strict liability (see pages 16–20).

Mens rea generally allows the blameworthy to be punished by distinguishing between those who commit the *actus reus* of an offence accidentally and those who take an unjustifiable risk of harm or who deliberately set out to commit a crime.

There are several types of *mens rea* and different crimes have different *mens rea* requirements. To be liable for theft, for example, the defendant must have acted dishonestly with the intention of permanently depriving the owner of his or her property. For murder, the defendant must have intended to kill or to cause serious harm. Two of the most commonly required types of *mens rea* are intention and recklessness.

1 *Intention*

Many crimes require that the defendant had the necessary intent when committing the offence. It is a subjective test that requires the court to establish what the defendant was actually thinking.

Intention is a word in common use but it has two distinct meanings in the context of *mens rea*: direct intention and indirect (oblique) intention.

1.1 Direct intention

Direct intention means that the defendant set out to achieve a particular result or consequence. It is sometimes explained by saying that the defendant foresaw a particular result as a certainty and wanted to bring it about. It was defined in *Moloney* (see below) as 'a true desire to bring about the consequences'. An example would be where the defendant shoots his victim in the chest because he wants to kill him.

1.2 Indirect/oblique intention

These are known as 'specific intent' crimes.

Many crimes require the prosecution to prove that when committing the *actus reus* the defendant was acting either intentionally or recklessly. For some crimes, however, the prosecution will not be able to rely on recklessness but will need to prove beyond reasonable doubt that the defendant intended to bring about the consequences. In this situation intention may still be proved using the definition of indirect/oblique intention.

Sometimes a defendant will claim that he or she did not intend the result and indeed did not want it to occur. If this is so, the defendant is not guilty and must be acquitted. The problem occurs, however, when the result was virtually certain to occur, although not desired for its own sake, and the defendant went ahead with his or her actions anyway. An example might be where a terrorist blows up a plane in order to kill one of the passengers. The terrorist may claim that he or she did not want to kill any of the passengers other than his or her intended target, but by blowing up a plane, it is a virtual certainty that all the passengers will be killed. The defendant could therefore be said to have intended their deaths if he or she knew that they were virtually certain to occur and, despite recognising this, was determined to continue. Not surprisingly, this issue has posed many problems, and a number of cases have come before the courts to determine the meaning of indirect intent.

R v *Moloney* (1985)

The defendant and the victim (his stepfather) had been drinking heavily. They decided to have a race to see who could load and fire a gun in the fastest time. Moloney was quicker and pointed the gun at his stepfather who challenged him to fire it. Moloney promptly did so, hitting his stepfather in the head and killing him. At trial, Moloney claimed that he never intended to kill the victim or even to cause him serious harm, arguing that he was just joking around. The House of Lords substituted his murder conviction for one of manslaughter, stating that only an intention to kill or to cause serious injury was sufficient for a murder charge. It said the jury should ask if death or serious injury was a natural consequence of the defendant's actions. If so, it should then go on to consider whether the defendant realised this. If it believed that the defendant *did* realise this, this was evidence from which the jury could infer that the defendant did have the required intent.

R v *Hancock and Shankland* (1986)

The defendants were Welsh coal miners on strike. When one of their fellow miners wanted to return to work, they tried to stop him. The 'strike-breaker' was driven in a taxi to another coal mine, and the route was via a motorway. The defendants knew that the taxi would pass under a particular bridge and when the taxi drove under it they pushed concrete blocks onto the road below. One of the blocks hit the windscreen of the taxi and the driver was killed. The defendants claimed that their only intention was to block the road and prevent the strike-breaker from reaching the coal mine, not to kill the driver of the taxi. The House of Lords substituted their murder convictions with manslaughter convictions. It emphasised that the probability or chance of the consequence occurring must be taken into account. The more probable the result, the more likely that the defendant foresaw it; and the more likely that the defendant foresaw it, the more likely he or she could be said to have intended it.

R v *Nedrick* (1986)

The defendant held a grudge against a woman and intended to frighten her by pushing a lighted substance through her letterbox. Fire broke out in the house and the woman's child was killed. After a misdirection by the trial judge, the Court of Appeal said that the jury should determine whether the defendant had the required intention by asking first how probable the consequence was and second whether the defendant foresaw the consequence. If death or serious bodily harm were virtually certain to occur, and the defendant appreciated this, then the jury could use this as evidence that he had the necessary intention.

***R* v *Woollin* (1998)**
The defendant lost his temper when his 3-month-old son started choking on his food. He picked him up, shook him and then threw him across the room towards his pram. The baby hit the wall instead and died as a result of his injuries. At trial, the defendant claimed that he had not intended to kill his son and had not wanted him to die. The judge told the jury that it could convict if it was satisfied that the defendant had seen a 'substantial risk' of serious injury. On appeal, the House of Lords confirmed that the consequence must be a virtually certain result of the defendant's actions and the defendant must appreciate this.

Indirect intent can be a difficult concept to understand at first, so you may need to read through this section several times.

In conclusion, direct intent is where the defendant actually wanted the result and indirect/oblique intent is where the defendant did not necessarily want the result but foresaw it to a point of virtual certainty and was determined to carry on anyway.

2 *Recklessness*

Another common type of *mens rea* is recklessness, which covers the situation where a defendant takes an unjustifiable risk. As with intention, it is a subjective test and the defendant must recognise the risk that he or she is running. Recklessness was defined in the case of *R* v *Cunningham*.

***R* v *Cunningham* (1957)**
In need of money, the defendant removed a gas meter from a wall in order to take the cash within it. Removing the meter allowed gas to escape and to enter the house next door, where his neighbour inhaled it and became ill. Cunningham was charged with 'maliciously administering a noxious thing so as to endanger life' contrary to s.23 of the **Offences Against The Person Act 1861**. The courts were asked to consider the meaning of the word 'malicious', which they stated did not require ill will or bad feeling but should simply be taken to mean that the defendant acted either intentionally or recklessly. They went on to say that recklessness required the defendant to foresee the chance or possibility of the result occurring. Thus, in order to be found guilty, Cunningham must have realised there was a risk that in acting as he did the gas might escape and endanger somebody's life, and, recognising that risk, he removed the meter anyway. He was, in fact, acquitted due to a misdirection.

There were previously two different types of recklessness, subjective and objective, but the objective form is now extinct following the case of *R* v *G*.

***R* v *G and Another* (2003)**
Two children aged 11 and 12 put lit newspaper under a wheelie-bin in a yard. The bin caught fire and the fire spread to shops and other nearby buildings, causing over £1 million of damage. The boys were charged with arson, but at their trial

they argued that they had not seen the risk that the fire might spread. The House of Lords applied the Cunningham test of subjective recklessness, and since the defendants had not appreciated the risk, they were not guilty of arson.

In conclusion, subjective recklessness is when the defendant foresees the result as a mere possibility — he or she did not necessarily desire the result but was prepared to take a chance. In other words, the defendant took an unjustifiable risk.

C Transferred malice

The defendant will generally be guilty if he or she has both the *actus reus* and *mens rea* of a crime. Sometimes, however, there may be an unexpected turn of events. For example, the defendant may intend to kill one person but make a mistake of identity and kill a different person instead. The defendant may argue that while the *actus reus* relates to the actual victim, there was no *mens rea*, as he or she intended to kill a completely different person. The courts are unwilling to find that the defendant is not guilty in such a situation and have therefore developed the doctrine of transferred malice. Under this doctrine, if the defendant with the *mens rea* of a crime causes the *actus reus* of the same crime, the *mens rea* or malice is simply transferred to the actual victim. This ensures that the defendant can be found guilty, even though the actual result was an unintended one.

***R* v *Latimer* (1886)**
During an argument in a pub, the defendant took off his belt and swung it at his intended victim. The belt hit a bystander instead, causing injury. Latimer was convicted of wounding, as the courts transferred his intention to hit the intended victim onto his actual victim, ensuring that he had both the *actus reus* and *mens rea* of the offence.

This is a popular topic in scenario questions.

The position changes, however, if the defendant with the *mens rea* of one crime commits the *actus reus* of another.

***R* v *Pembliton* (1874)**
During a fight outside a pub, the defendant threw a stone into a crowd of people, intending to injure them. Instead, the stone missed and smashed a window. The defendant was convicted of malicious damage but this was quashed on appeal. The defendant had committed the *actus reus* of malicious damage but had the *mens rea* of assault, and since it was a completely different crime, the *mens rea* could not be transferred.

D Contemporaneity

The general rule is that to be guilty of a crime, a defendant must have the *actus reus* and *mens rea* at the same time. In some circumstances, this could lead to criminals being acquitted, so the courts have developed ways of dealing with such cases.

1 Continuing act

In situations where the *actus reus* comes first, the courts apply the 'continuing act' doctrine, where the *actus reus* is stretched over time to meet the point where the defendant had *mens rea*.

***Fagan* v *MPC* (1969)**
While parking his car, the defendant accidentally drove over a policeman's foot. He then refused to move and switched off the engine. When charged with assault, Fagan tried to argue that he did not have the *actus reus* and *mens rea* at the same time. He claimed that the *actus reus* occurred when he drove onto the foot but he had no *mens rea* at the time, as it was an accident. He later developed an intention to remain on the foot but claimed that the *actus reus* was complete by then. The courts did not accept his argument and his appeal was rejected. It was held that driving onto the foot and remaining there was a continuing act and it was enough that Fagan had *mens rea* at some point during it.

2 One transaction

Look out for these scenarios as they are commonly used in problem questions.

In some cases, the *mens rea* may come first. In this situation, the courts apply the 'one transaction' doctrine. This can occur when the defendant hits the victim and knocks him or her unconscious. The defendant might assume that the victim is in fact dead rather than unconscious and then try to dispose of the body. The victim is actually killed during the disposal process.

***Thabo Meli* v *R* (1954)**
The defendants set out to kill their victim and decided that they would hit him over the head and then push his body off a cliff to make it look like he had died in an accident. They put their plan into action, and after hitting him, pushed what they thought was his dead body over the cliff. However, the victim was unconscious rather than dead but later died from the fall and exposure. The defendants claimed that they had the requisite *mens rea* when they hit him over the head but by the time the *actus reus* occurred and the victim actually died, they no longer had *mens rea* as they had thought that he was already dead. The Privy Council held that, since it was all part of the same series of events, it was a single transaction during which time the defendants had both *actus reus* and *mens rea*.

E Strict liability

1 Definition

There is no requirement to prove *mens rea* in strict liability offences — they are complete when the defendant performs the *actus reus*. This means that a defendant who did not intend to commit such a crime is still liable, no matter how carefully he or she has tried to avoid the outcome. For example, a defendant who has been spiked with drink or drugs will still be liable for driving while unfit, even though he or she has no *mens rea*.

Consider whether you think that this was a fair outcome.

***Callow* v *Tillstone* (1900)**
The defendant was a butcher who asked a vet to check whether or not a carcass was fit for human consumption. The vet said it was fit for sale, but he had been negligent and in fact the meat was unfit. The defendant was guilty of offering unfit meat for sale, even though he had taken all reasonable precautions to avoid doing so.

2 Types of offence

2.1 Common law

Generally, the courts are not in favour of strict liability offences, preferring an element of fault before imposing criminal liability. Thus, most strict liability crimes are statutory in origin. There are some examples, however, of strict liability in common law.

2.1a Blasphemous libel

***Whitehouse* v *Lemon and Gay News* (1979)**
In 1976, *Gay News* published a poem linking Jesus with homosexual acts. Mary Whitehouse, a campaigner for morals and standards in the media, brought a private prosecution against the publishers of the magazine and its editor, Denis Lemon. The offence alleged was 'blasphemous libel' due to the obscene nature of the poem. The question was whether the defendants needed to have intended to commit blasphemy. The House of Lords held that this was not needed — it was enough to convict if the words were blasphemous and the editor and publishers intended to print them. They need not have intended to offend people, as whether the words were blasphemous was a strict liability offence.

2.2 Regulatory offences

If the offence is not one where a moral issue may be at stake, the courts are more willing to dispense with the need for *mens rea*. Such offences include food regulations, where the penalties are small and the removal of the requirement to prove *mens rea* makes them much easier to enforce.

***Smedleys* v *Breed* (1974)**
The defendants were convicted when a caterpillar was found in a tin of peas produced in their factory. They had taken all reasonable precautions to avoid contamination, but despite this the House of Lords upheld the conviction.

Many road traffic offences, including drink driving and speeding, are strict liability in nature.

***R* v *Bosher* (1973)**
The defendant was convicted of driving while disqualified. His defence was that he believed his disqualification had ended, especially since his licence had been sent back to him. Despite his reasonable belief, he was convicted.

In *Sweet* v *Parsley*, the courts gave guidance on the distinction between true crimes and regulatory offences.

Being convicted of a drugs-related offence obviously carries a social stigma — particularly if the defendant is a teacher, as in this case.

***Sweet* v *Parsley* (1970)**
A teacher rented out her farmhouse to students who smoked cannabis on the premises. She was completely unaware of this since she did not spend much time there. When the police raided the house and found the drugs, she was charged with 'being concerned in the management of premises used for the purposes of smoking cannabis'. She was eventually acquitted on appeal when the House of Lords held that any crime to which social stigma was attached should normally require *mens rea*.

3 *Public welfare*

Use the examples given to illustrate this point in an essay.

Businesses are often subject to strict liability offences. This is to ensure that high standards of care are taken in order to protect public welfare.

***Harrow LBC* v *Shah* (1999)**
A shop owner was held liable when an employee sold a lottery ticket to someone aged under 16. The assistant had reasonably thought the customer to be above the age limit, but despite this the conviction stood.

***Alphacell Ltd* v *Woodward* (1972)**
Alphacell Ltd was prosecuted under the **Rivers (Prevention of Pollution) Act 1951** when dirty water from its factory entered a river. The relevant words of the statute were 'causes or knowingly permits to enter a stream any poisonous, noxious or polluting matter'. The question was whether the company had 'caused' the matter to enter the river. It argued that it had a system in place to try to ensure that the stream was not polluted, but it was still liable under the Act. It was held that 'causing' did not require proof of *mens rea*.

***R* v *Blake* (1997)**
The defendant was charged with broadcasting without a licence under the **Wireless Telegraphy Act 1949**. The Court of Appeal held that it was a strict liability offence, as unlicensed radio broadcasts could interfere with emergency-service radio communications.

4 *How the courts decide*

4.1 Wording of the Act

It is not always clear when an offence is one of strict liability. Sometimes the wording of an Act makes it clear. Words such as 'knowingly, 'intentionally' and 'recklessly' all indicate that *mens rea* is required. If Parliament has not included any of these words in a statute, then it suggests that it intended the offence to be one of strict liability. This also applies if Parliament has included *mens rea* words in other sections of the statute but not the one in question.

***James and Son* v *Smee* (1955)**
The motor vehicles regulations made it an offence to 'use, cause or permit to be used' a vehicle with defective brakes. The question was whether the defendant had 'permitted' the use of the vehicle in question. The actual user of the car was held strictly liable but the offence of permitting was held to require proof of the defendant's state of mind.

***Cundy* v *Le Cocq* (1884)**

The defendant was a landlord who was accused of an offence under the Licensing Act when he sold alcohol to someone who was already drunk. The defendant did not know that the person was drunk but it was held to be a strict liability offence. Other parts of the statute included *mens rea* words, but the relevant section did not. The courts therefore presumed that Parliament had not required the defendant to possess *mens rea* before he could be convicted.

There is always a presumption that *mens rea* is necessary for conviction of a criminal offence. This can be rebutted, however, with a 'compellingly clear' implication that Parliament intended otherwise.

4.2 The *Gammon* propositions

In the case of *Gammon* v *Attorney General of Hong Kong*, the courts gave guidance as to when a crime would be regarded as one of strict liability.

***Gammon Ltd* v *Attorney General of Hong Kong* (1985)**

The defendants were carrying out building work in Hong Kong. Part of the building collapsed due to the builders' failure to follow their original plans. Regulations in Hong Kong made it an offence to change building plans substantially, and the defendants were charged. They argued that they did not know their deviation was 'substantial'. The Privy Council held it was an offence of strict liability and gave guidance on how such decisions were made.

The courts presume that *mens rea* is required in criminal cases, particularly if the offence is 'truly criminal'. The presumption applies to statutory offences and can only be rebutted if the statute states that the offence is one of strict liability or there is clear implication that this is the case. The presumption can only be displaced when the statute deals with a matter of social concern, and only then if strict liability will assist in preventing it.

5 Evaluation

5.1 Arguments in favour of strict liability

There are several arguments in favour of strict liability:

- Strict liability offences encourage **high standards of care**, since a potential defendant is aware that he or she will face certain conviction if the offence is committed. It is argued that this protects the public from potential harm. It also acts as a deterrent to would-be offenders.
- It is **easier to obtain convictions**. Strict liability removes the need to prove *mens rea*, which is often difficult.
- The **punishments for such offences are generally small** and there is usually no risk of going to prison.

Ensure that you can produce a balanced response to a question asking about the advantages and disadvantages of strict liability.

5.2 Arguments against strict liability

There are also several arguments against strict liability offences:

- Critics argue that such offences **lead to injustice**, when a defendant has taken all reasonable steps to avoid committing the offence but is still convicted.

- It **may not act as a deterrent**, as potential offenders are more likely to be concerned about the chances of actually being caught.
- Opponents say that it may be **too easy to obtain convictions** and the need for *mens rea* should not be dispensed with simply to make cases easier for the prosecution.
- The **penalties for such offences are not always small**, and those convicted may well face prison sentences. In *Gammon*, the maximum penalty was 3 years' imprisonment and/or a large fine.

In addition, sentencing is more difficult since all defendants have committed the *actus reus*, and without *mens rea* evidence it is difficult to distinguish between the deliberate and the accidental offender.

6 *Reform*

It has been suggested that the defence of 'due diligence' should be allowed for strict liability offences. This would mean that the defendant would not be liable if he or she could show, on the balance of probabilities, that he or she took all reasonable steps to avoid committing the offence.

F Absolute liability

Make sure that you understand the difference between strict liability and absolute liability offences.

Absolute liability is an offence that does not require a *mens rea* and the *actus reus* need not be performed voluntarily. If an offence is one of absolute liability, the defendant will be liable if he or she performed the *actus reus*. Unlike strict liability, the prosecution does not need to prove that the defendant was acting voluntarily, so even an involuntary act would incur liability. Few offences fall into this category, and those that do must be clearly defined as such. *R* v *Larsonneur* (1933) and *Winzar* v *Chief Constable of Kent* (1983) are both examples of absolute liability (see page 9).

Summary of Topic 1

Actus reus

Actus reus is Latin for 'guilty act'. The *actus reus* is made up of all of the parts of the crime except the defendant's mental state. There are several different types of *actus reus*. The general rule is that in order to be liable, the defendant's conduct must be voluntary, e.g. *Leicester* v *Pearson* (1952).

Conduct crimes

The *actus reus* is simply prohibited conduct.

Omissions as *actus reus*

An omission is a failure to do something. The general rule in criminal law is that a person is not usually liable for his or her omissions. However, there are several different circumstances that will give rise to a duty to act.

Duty arising from specific relationships
Parents owe a duty to look after their children and may be prosecuted if they fail to do so, e.g. *R* v *Gibbins and Proctor* (1918).

Duty arising from a contract
If a defendant is under a contractual duty to act and fails to do so, he or she may be liable if others are likely to be injured as a result, e.g. *R* v *Pittwood* (1902).

Duty through public office
e.g. *R* v *Dytham* (1979)

Voluntary assumption of a duty
e.g. *R* v *Stone and Dobinson* (1977)

Duty arising from dangerous prior conduct
e.g. *R* v *Miller* (1983)

State of affairs crimes
The *actus reus* involves 'being' rather than 'doing' — it is the circumstances that create the offence, e.g. *R* v *Larsonneur* (1933) and *Winzar* v *Chief Constable of Kent* (1983).

Result crimes
The prosecution must prove that the defendant's actions caused the prohibited result. In order to establish this, it must prove a causal link between the action and the consequence.

Factual causation
The test for factual causation is the 'but for' test — but for the defendant's actions, would the victim have suffered harm? If not, then the test is satisfied (*R* v *White*, 1910).

Legal causation
The test for legal causation is whether the defendant's conduct made a 'significant contribution' to the result. The chain of causation may be affected by a number of factors:

- The **actions of the victim** may break the chain of causation, but only if they are unreasonable (*R* v *Roberts*, 1978).
- The **actions of a third party** may break the chain of causation, but as with actions of the victim, they will not if they are reasonably foreseeable (e.g. *R* v *Pagett*, 1983). If the victim has received negligent medical treatment, this will not break the chain of causation unless it is 'palpably wrong' (*R* v *Jordan*, 1956). Switching off a life-support machine will not break the chain of causation (*R* v *Malcherek and Steel*, 1981).
- The **'thin-skull' test** — if some pre-existing weakness or medical condition of the victim makes the result of an attack more severe than it would be ordinarily, the defendant cannot argue that the chain of causation has been broken (*R* v *Blaue*, 1975).

Mens rea

Mens rea is Latin for 'guilty mind' and concerns the criminal intention of the defendant when the *actus reus* was committed. There are several types of *mens rea* and different crimes have different *mens rea* requirements. Two of the most commonly required types of *mens rea* are intention and recklessness.

Intention

Many crimes require that the defendant had the necessary intent when committing the offence. It is a subjective test that requires the court to establish what the defendant was thinking. Intention is a word in common use but it has two distinct meanings in the context of *mens rea*: direct intention and indirect/oblique intention (*R* v *Moloney*, 1985, *R* v *Nedrick*, 1986 and *R* v *Woollin*, 1998).

Recklessness

Recklessness was defined in the case of *R* v *Cunningham*. There were previously two different types of recklessness — subjective and objective — but the objective form is now extinct following the case of *R* v *G* (2003).

Transferred malice

Under this doctrine, if the defendant with the *mens rea* of a crime causes the *actus reus* of the same crime to a different victim, the *mens rea* or malice is simply transferred to the actual victim. This ensures that the defendant can be found guilty even though the actual result was unintended, e.g. *R* v *Latimer* (1886) and *R* v *Pembliton* (1874).

Contemporaneity

The general rule is that in order to be guilty of a crime, a defendant must have the *actus reus* and *mens rea* at the same time.

Continuing act

In situations where the *actus reus* comes first, the courts apply the 'continuing act' doctrine, where the *actus reus* is stretched over time to meet the point where the defendant had *mens rea*, e.g. *Fagan* v *MPC* (1969).

One transaction

If the *actus reus* and *mens rea* are part of a plan, the court will establish contemporaneity, e.g. *Thabo Meli* v *R* (1954).

Strict liability

There is no requirement to prove *mens rea* in strict liability offences — they are complete when the defendant performs the *actus reus*, e.g. *Callow* v *Tillstone* (1900).

Types of offence

- the Gammon propositions
- regulatory offences (e.g. *Smedleys* v *Breed*, 1974 and *Sweet* v *Parsley*, 1970)
- public welfare (*Harrow LBC* v *Shah*, 1999)

Evaluation

Advantages of strict liability include:

- encouragement of high standards
- no need to prove a *mens rea*
- punishments are small
- acts as a deterrent

Disadvantages of strict liability include:

- injustice
- easy to convict
- some strict liability crimes incur a large penalty
- not always a deterrent

Reform

It has been suggested that the defence of 'due diligence' should be allowed for strict liability offences.

Absolute liability

If an offence is one of absolute liability, the defendant will be liable if he or she performed the *actus reus*. Unlike strict liability, the prosecution does not need to prove that the defendant was acting voluntarily.

TOPIC 2 Murder

Murder is a homicide offence, a category that also encompasses voluntary and involuntary manslaughter — essentially offences where the defendant has caused the death of the victim.

A Definition

Murder is a common-law offence, so remember that there is no statute defining it.

Unlike most crimes, murder is still a common-law offence, and as such there is no statute that defines the conduct required. This may seem strange for such a serious crime, but the necessary elements can be determined by considering the development of the law through a number of leading cases.

1 Coke's definition

Use this definition in the introduction of an essay on murder.

As a starting point, it is commonly accepted that Sir Edward Coke gave the classic definition of murder in his work *Institutes of the Laws of England*, published in 1797:

> Murder is when a man of sound memory, and of the age of discretion, unlawfully killeth within any country of the realm any reasonable creature *in rerum natura* under the King's peace, with malice aforethought, either expressed by the party or implied by law, so as the party wounded or hurt die of the wound or hurt, within a year and a day after the same.

B *Actus reus*

In a problem question dealing with murder, explain each of these six requirements in turn and then apply the facts before concluding whether the defendant has committed the *actus reus*.

The various elements that make up the *actus reus* of murder can be discovered from Coke's definition.

1 Of sound memory and of the age of discretion

As with other crimes, the defendant must be sane and aged 10 years or over.

2 Unlawfully killeth

Certain defences may make a killing lawful, for example self-defence (see Topic 7). Defences aside, this part of the definition has been taken to mean 'cause the death of'. Murder is a result crime, and as such the prosecution must prove beyond reasonable doubt that the defendant's conduct caused the victim's death. It must prove both factual and legal causation (see Topic 1).

3 Within any country of the realm

If the defendant is a British citizen, he or she can be tried in the UK for murder committed in another country.

4 *Any reasonable creature in* rerum natura

This is understood to mean a person who is born and not dead (*rerum natura* means 'capable of living'). This seems straightforward at first glance, but the exact timing of the beginning and end of life can cause problems. Generally, the beginning of life is taken to be when a baby has an existence independent of its mother. Therefore, if someone attacks a pregnant woman and the baby dies in the womb, it cannot be murder because the baby is not considered to be a person in being. However, note also the following case of Attorney General's Reference No. 3 (1994).

***Attorney General's Reference No. 3* (1994)**
The defendant stabbed his pregnant girlfriend in the abdomen. The baby was born prematurely and later died. The question was whether the defendant could be convicted of the murder of the child. The House of Lords held that the fact that the child had not yet been born at the time of the attack did not prevent a murder conviction when it later died. On the facts, however, it was not possible to transfer the malice (the intention to cause grievous bodily harm to the mother) to make the defendant liable for the murder of the baby. At best, a conviction for manslaughter was a possibility.

The end of life can also be difficult to determine. There is no legal definition, but generally brain-stem death is accepted as signalling the end of life. The case of *R* v *Malcherek and Steel* (1981) was covered in Topic 1. The two cases were joined on appeal, since the same point was at issue in each. In both cases, death was said to follow brain-stem death.

A defendant who tries to kill someone who, unbeknown to him or her, is already dead will not be guilty of murder but may be liable for attempt (see Topic 12).

5 *Under the King's peace*

Obviously, today it is 'under the Queen's peace', but it amounts to the same meaning in each case. Killing another would not amount to murder if that person were an enemy during wartime.

6 *So that the party wounded or hurt die within a year and a day*

The requirement that the victim must die of his or her injuries within a year and a day was understandable in previous times, when long breaks between the defendant's conduct and the victim's death would make it difficult for the prosecution to prove causation. Following modern advances in medical technology, however, doctors are able to keep patients alive for much longer periods. A number of cases highlighted the unfairness of the rule, whereby a defendant was able to escape liability for murder simply because the victim took longer than a year and a day to die. It was finally abolished by the **Law Reform (Year and a Day Rule) Act 1996**.

To avoid a situation where the defendant is uncertain about possible charges as the prosecution waits to see if the victim will die, any case with a gap of more than 3 years between the defendant's conduct and the death of the victim requires the permission of the Attorney General. Similarly, if the defendant has already been prosecuted in relation to the incident — probably for a non-fatal offence — the Attorney General's consent will be required.

C *Mens rea*

The *mens rea* of murder is malice aforethought. This means that the defendant must either intend to kill or intend to cause grievous bodily harm (GBH). The phrase is misleading, since in this context 'malice' does not mean ill will, and premeditation is not necessary. The person who acts on the spur of the moment or the doctor who carries out euthanasia are equally as guilty as the cold-blooded killer.

The fact that the *mens rea* of murder can be satisfied by an intention to cause grievous bodily harm has been strongly criticised. Opponents say it is unfair to find a defendant guilty of murder when he or she did not intend or even foresee loss of life. Others suggest that if the defendant intentionally sets out to cause really serious harm, then he or she must face the consequences of his or her actions, however severe they may be.

It is now settled law that both direct and indirect intention will satisfy the *mens rea* requirement, but it took a number of cases to determine this issue.

***Hyam* v *DPP* (1975)**
The defendant put a burning newspaper through the letterbox of a woman she wanted to frighten. The victim's two children were killed in the resulting fire. The defendant insisted that she had intended merely to frighten the victim, and not to cause death. The court held that Hyam must have foreseen death or grievous bodily harm as a highly likely consequence of her actions, and was therefore guilty of murder. The case was heavily criticised in subsequent cases, as it appeared to suggest that the *mens rea* for murder would be satisfied by the defendant who foresaw the consequences. Thus, intention was taken to be the same as foresight of the consequences. In other words, a defendant who foresees what is likely to happen will always be taken to have intended the consequences.

Following criticism of *Hyam*, the meaning of intention was again considered in *Moloney* (1985) (see page 13). Here, the House of Lords decided that the decision in *Hyam* was wrong and it was overturned. Foresight does not automatically mean that the defendant has the necessary intention — it is merely evidence of it. *Hancock and Shankland* followed in 1986, and the House of Lords again decided that foresight of consequences is only evidence of intention. In *R* v *Nedrick* (1986) (see pages 13–14), the question arose as to how likely a consequence needs to be before a defendant may be said to have intended it. The Court of Appeal decided that if the defendant realises that death or GBH would be a 'virtually certain' result of his or her conduct, then the jury may find that he or she intended to cause the result. Again, this would only be evidence of intention and a jury would not be obliged to find the defendant guilty. Finally, in 1998 the House of Lords confirmed that the test in *Nedrick* of 'virtual certainty' was the correct one to use in the leading case of *Woollin*.

***R* v *Matthews and Alleyne* (2003)**
The two defendants robbed the victim and then pushed him off a bridge into a river, despite the victim's protestations that he was unable to swim. Both defendants claimed that they lacked the necessary *mens rea* for murder — they had not intended to kill their victim. The judge directed the jury that if the defendants appreciated that drowning was a virtual certainty then they must have had the intention to kill him. On appeal, it was stressed that even if the defendant does foresee death or GBH as a virtual certainty, the jury may find intention but it does not have to. It is simply a rule of evidence rather than of law and it is something that a jury may use to help it to decide whether or not the defendant had the necessary intention.

D Evaluation

Mention any relevant reports in your answer to gain more marks.

In July 2005, the government announced a review of the current homicide law and the Law Commission issued a consultation paper entitled 'A New Homicide Act for England and Wales?' (Consultation Paper No. 177). The paper examines some of the problems with the current law and suggests possible reforms to counteract them.

1 *Lack of cohesion*

In the paper, the current homicide law is described as 'a rickety structure set upon shaky foundations'. One problem is that parts of the current law have been in existence for centuries and have barely changed in that time to reflect current thinking. Other parts have changed a number of times over the years and this has led to uncertainty. The main issue is that murder is a common-law offence developed through decisions in many cases over long periods of time. These cases have in turn led to uncertainty and ambiguities, which required further cases to settle. Critics argue that it is essential to have a clear definition of murder, the most serious of criminal offences.

2 *Problems with* mens rea

2.1 Intention

A succession of cases have highlighted the uncertainty over the *mens rea* of murder. *Hyam*, *Moloney*, *Nedrick* and *Woollin* brought to attention the difficulties that the courts have faced in establishing the meaning of intention. Currently, cases like *Matthews and Alleyne* highlight that the guidance given to juries is a rule of evidence rather than a rule of law. This means that, despite the numerous cases on the subject, there is still no clear definition of intention, and since existing rules are rules of evidence rather than law, juries may make different decisions in cases with similar facts.

2.2 Intention to cause grievous bodily harm

The *mens rea* of murder can be satisfied when the defendant intends only to cause GBH. This has led to great debate over whether someone should be convicted of murder when he or she had no intention of causing death or had not even considered the possibility that it may occur.

3 *Life sentence*

The mandatory sentence for murder is life imprisonment. The compulsory nature of the sentence has been criticised, as it does not allow judges the flexibility to pass sentences appropriate to the circumstances of the case. The defendant who commits the mercy killing of a terminally ill relative will receive the same sentence as the defendant who kills in cold blood.

E Reform

1 *Legislation: passing a new Homicide Act*

The Law Commission has proposed that the ambiguities surrounding the law on murder should be resolved through legislation, namely a new Homicide Act. This would, it hopes, achieve the certainty that has been lacking in this area for so long. The new Act would encompass all of the elements of homicide — murder, voluntary manslaughter and involuntary manslaughter. The Law Commission suggests that the offences should be defined according to a 'ladder principle' or hierarchy, which reflects the seriousness of the various offences.

Murder would be divided into 'first-degree' and 'second-degree' categories:

- First-degree murder would apply to the defendant who intended to kill, and he or she would receive the mandatory life sentence.
- Second-degree murder would carry a discretionary life sentence and would apply to defendants who:
  - killed while intending to commit serious harm
  - were 'recklessly indifferent' to causing death — when they saw the risk of killing they carried on with their conduct without caring whether death would occur
  - rely on provocation, diminished responsibility or duress as a defence

The new Act would also include a clear definition of the *mens rea* required for murder — particularly regarding intention. It is hoped that this would solve the current problems faced by the courts in this sphere.

2 Abolition of the mandatory life sentence

It has been suggested that the compulsory nature of the sentence should be changed, so that the maximum sentence remains life imprisonment but judges are free to sentence according to the circumstances of each case rather than being restrained by a mandatory sentence.

Summary of Topic 2

Coke's definition

> Murder is when a man of sound memory, and of the age of discretion, unlawfully killeth within any country of the realm any reasonable creature *in rerum natura* under the King's peace, with malice aforethought, either expressed by the party or implied by law, so as the party wounded or hurt die of the wound or hurt, within a year and a day after the same.

Actus reus

- Murder is committed when a person unlawfully kills a human being under the Queen's peace.
- The defendant must be sane and aged 10 years or over.
- The victim must be a human who is born and not dead.
- The rules on factual and legal causation apply — the defendant must cause the death of the victim.
- The old rule that the victim must die within a year and a day was abolished by the **Law Reform (Year and a Day Rule) Act 1996**.

Mens rea

Mens rea is defined as malice aforethought. This means either an intention to kill or an intention to cause grievous bodily harm. The defendant may have direct or indirect intention.

Evaluation

Lack of cohesion

Murder is a common-law offence developed through decisions in many cases over long periods of time. These cases have in turn led to uncertainty and ambiguities, which required further cases to settle. Critics argue that it is essential to have a clear definition of murder, as it is the most serious of all criminal offences.

Problems with *mens rea*

- Cases like *Hyam*, *Moloney*, *Nedrick* and *Woollin* highlight the difficulties that the courts have faced in establishing the meaning of intention, and even today there is still no clear definition. This means that juries may make different decisions in cases with similar facts.
- The *mens rea* of murder can be satisfied when the defendant intends only to cause GBH, which means that a defendant could be convicted of murder when he or she did not have any intention of causing death or had not even considered the possibility that it may occur.

Life sentence

The mandatory life sentence for murder has been criticised, as it does not allow judges the flexibility to pass sentences appropriate to the circumstances of individual cases.

Reform

Passing a new Homicide Act

The Law Commission has proposed that the ambiguities surrounding the law of murder should be resolved through legislation, namely a new Homicide Act. Murder would be divided into 'first-degree' and 'second-degree' categories.

Abolition of the mandatory life sentence

It has been suggested that judges should be free to sentence according to the circumstances of each case, rather that being restrained by a mandatory life sentence.

TOPIC 3 Voluntary manslaughter

Don't forget that the defendant must have the *actus reus* and *mens rea* of murder before these defences apply.

All three defences are known as 'special defences', as they apply only to murder. They are also *partial* defences, as the defendant is still found guilty of manslaughter.

Voluntary manslaughter was introduced by Parliament via the **Homicide Act 1957**. It was designed to cover the situation where the defendant has both the *actus reus* and *mens rea* of murder but the surrounding circumstances of the offence mean that the defendant's liability is reduced from murder to manslaughter. These circumstances amount to partial defences specific to a murder charge and are defined by the Homicide Act as:

- diminished responsibility
- provocation
- suicide pacts

The defendant will not be charged with voluntary manslaughter but with murder, to which he or she will plead the relevant defence. If successful, he or she will then be convicted of manslaughter.

A Diminished responsibility

1 *Definition*

Diminished responsibility is defined in s.2 of the **Homicide Act 1957**:

> Where a person kills or is party to a killing of another, he shall not be convicted of murder if he was suffering from such abnormality of mind (whether arising from a condition of arrested or retarded development of mind or any inherent causes or induced by disease or injury) as substantially impaired his mental responsibility for his acts and omissions in doing or being a party to the killing.

2 *Elements*

2.1 Abnormality of mind

The definition of 'abnormality of mind' comes from the case of *R* v *Byrne* (1960), when Lord Parker described it as a state of mind so different from that of ordinary people that the reasonable person would term it abnormal. This is a matter for the jury to decide in each case, based on the medical evidence submitted by both the defence and the prosecution.

***R* v *Byrne* (1960)**

The defendant strangled his victim in a hostel and then mutilated her body. He claimed that he was unable to control his perverted sexual desires and had acted under an irresistible impulse. The original trial judge directed the jury that diminished responsibility was not relevant in this case. The Court of Appeal held that the term 'abnormality of mind' covered all aspects of the mind, including the ability to control physical acts as well as the ability to make rational decisions. Byrne's conviction was reduced to manslaughter.

2.2 Arising from a cause specified in the Act

The definition in s.2 of the Act specifies that the abnormality of mind must arise from a condition of arrested or retarded development of mind or any inherent cause or be induced by disease or injury.

2.2a A condition of arrested or retarded development of mind

This covers mental deficiencies.

2.2b Any inherent cause

An inherent cause is something internal and covers a wide variety of situations. The courts have accepted various conditions as being inherent causes, including epilepsy, premenstrual tension, battered-wife syndrome and shock. Depression due to a chemical imbalance in the brain is acceptable, but not if it is caused by a reaction to an event, as this would be an external cause.

2.2c Induced by disease or injury

'Disease' has been held to cover both physical and mental disease. Injuries include things such as brain damage caused by being hit on the head.

Drink or drugs will not usually give rise to an abnormality of mind, unless they have caused brain damage.

R v *Tandy* (1989)

The defendant was an alcoholic who strangled her 11-year-old daughter after the child had told her that the defendant's husband was abusing her. The defendant stated that she was able to exercise a degree of control over her drinking and her appeal against conviction was dismissed. To rely on diminished responsibility, the abnormality of the mind had to be induced by disease or injury. The defendant had not demonstrated that her brain was damaged so she could not rely on 'injury'. In terms of disease, in order to rely on an abnormality of mind induced by alcoholism, the defendant had to show that her drinking was involuntary. As she admitted to having some control over her cravings and as her first drink of the day was voluntary, she was not able to rely on the defence.

2.3 Substantial impairment of the defendant's mental responsibility

The abnormality of mind must have substantially impaired the defendant's mental responsibility for his or her acts and omissions. Again, this will be a matter for the jury to decide. The use of the word 'substantial' indicates that the impairment need not be absolute, so the defendant is without any responsibility, but it must be more than minimal. Thus the defendant who knows what he or she is doing but who finds it extremely difficult to control his or her actions will be covered by the defence.

2.4 Abnormality need not be the sole cause of the defendant's actions

In the case of *Dietschmann* (2003), the House of Lords held that a defendant might be able to rely on the defence of diminished responsibility despite being intoxicated, as long as the abnormality of mind was still a substantial cause of the killing. Juries will be directed to ignore the effect of any drugs or alcohol consumed by the defendant and will be told to consider whether, despite these, the defendant was still suffering from an abnormality of mind that substantially impaired his or her mental responsibility for the killing.

***R* v *Dietschmann* (2003)**
The defendant had been in a relationship with his aunt and suffered from depression when she died. After drinking heavily, the defendant attacked his victim as he believed he had broken his watch — a gift from his dead aunt. At his trial, the question arose as to whether the defendant could rely on the defence of diminished responsibility, despite the fact that he had been drinking. The House of Lords held that although drink could not be taken into account when considering his mental abnormality, it might have been the case that the defendant's mental abnormality and alcohol both had a part in impairing his mental responsibility. If so, it is up to the jury to decide whether, despite the drink, his mental abnormality substantially impaired his mental responsibility for his actions. If this is the case, the defence would still be available, despite the fact that he would not have killed had he been sober.

3 Burden and standard of proof

The defendant must prove, on the balance of probabilities, that he or she was suffering from diminished responsibility at the time of the killing. Medical evidence will be required from at least two experts to substantiate any such claim.

4 Effect

If pleaded successfully, the defence of diminished responsibility will reduce the defendant's liability from murder to that of manslaughter and thus allow him or her to avoid the mandatory life sentence.

5 Evaluation

The Law Commission recently reviewed the area of voluntary manslaughter in its paper 'Partial Defences to Murder' (Consultation Paper No. 173).

5.1 Meaning unclear

Critics argue that it is unclear precisely what the term 'diminished responsibility' means. There is little to assist in determining what constitutes an 'abnormality of mind' — it is simply defined as a state of mind that is 'abnormal'. There are also difficulties in trying to determine whether the defendant's mental responsibility has been 'substantially impaired'.

5.2 Burden of proof rests with the defendant

Opponents of the current law say that the burden of proof should be changed so that the onus is on the prosecution. This was suggested under the Draft Criminal Code.

5.3 Defines those in abusive relationships as mentally abnormal

In order to rely on the defence of diminished responsibility, those in abusive relationships who kill their abusers must claim to be mentally abnormal. Critics say that this should not be the case, and far more emphasis should be placed on the abuse that they have suffered rather than their state of mind.

5.4 Courts too ready to accept the defence in some cases

The courts have been criticised for being too willing to accept the defence of diminished responsibility in some instances. In a number of cases involving euthanasia, the courts may take the view that the defendant does not deserve to be labelled a murderer and face the accompanying life sentence, and so accept a plea of diminished responsibility on the basis of little evidence. Despite their good intentions, this is seen by many as a misuse of diminished responsibility.

***R* v *Heginbotham* (2004)**
The defendant in this case was 100 years old and was charged with the murder of his wife after he cut her throat. Before her death, she had been due to be moved to a different nursing home, but her husband felt that she would not receive the care that she needed there. He decided to kill her as an act of mercy in order to end her suffering. He was able to rely on diminished responsibility, despite not strictly meeting its requirements, and was sentenced to 12 months' community rehabilitation.

6 *Reform*

In its recent review, the Law Commission found that there had been a fall in the successful use of the diminished responsibility defence. However, it stated that the defence appeared to be working and advocated its retention as long as the mandatory life sentence for murder remains. No radical changes were proposed.

B Provocation

Provocation has long been recognised in common law as a partial defence to murder and may be seen as a concession to human frailty. Provocation is viewed as a factor that reduces the defendant's culpability.

1 *Definition*

Provocation is defined in s.3 of the **Homicide Act 1957**:

> Where on a charge of murder there is evidence on which the jury can find that the person charged was provoked (whether by things done or by things said or by both together) to lose his self-control, the question whether the provocation was enough to make a reasonable man do as he did shall be left to be determined by the jury; and in determining that question the jury shall take into account everything both done and said according to the effect which, in their opinion, it would have on a reasonable man.

2 Elements

2.1 Evidence of provocation

The judge must initially decide whether there is enough evidence of provocation to leave the defence to the jury. The defence need not be raised by the defendant personally but may still be left to the jury if there is sufficient evidence. Under s.3 of the Act, provocation may be caused by things said or things done, or both together. There is no requirement that such things are illegal.

***R* v *Doughty* (1986)**
The crying of a young baby amounted to provocation when his father killed him, despite the fact that it is perfectly normal for babies to cry.

The provocation need not be directed at the defendant or indeed may come from someone other than the victim.

***R* v *Pearson* (1992)**
Two brothers killed their father, who had been abusing the younger of the two. The Court of Appeal held that the jury should have been told to take into account the abuse when deciding whether the older brother had been provoked, despite the fact that the abuse was not aimed at him.

2.2 Test for provocation

The test for provocation encompasses an objective and subjective element.

Subjective tests are concerned with what the defendant did.

2.2a Subjective test

The first question that the jury must ask is whether, as a matter of fact, the defendant was provoked to lose his or her self-control.

***R* v *Miao* (2003)**
The defendant denied losing his self-control when he killed his girlfriend, despite the fact that a reasonable person may have done so in the same circumstances. The Court of Appeal held that there was insufficient evidence of provocation and as such the trial judge was correct not to leave the defence for the jury to consider.

It was held in *Duffy* (1949) that the loss of self-control must be 'sudden and temporary'. This requirement is in order to avoid bringing killings carried out in revenge under the scope of the defence. Pre-planned attacks are not the same as provocation.

***R* v *Ibrams and Gregory* (1981)**
The victim had been terrorising the defendants, who had sought but had not received protection from the police. The defendants made a plan to attack the victim a few days later. They planned to break his arms and legs but the victim subsequently died from injuries sustained in the attack. On appeal, their convictions were upheld since there was no evidence of a 'sudden and temporary' loss of self-control during the pre-planned attack.

***R* v *Cocker* (1989)**
The defendant killed his wife, who was suffering from a terminal disease. She had asked him repeatedly to suffocate her with a pillow. At his murder trial, he tried to

rely on her repeated requests to end her life as provocation. On appeal, his conviction was upheld, as the Court of Appeal did not consider that there had been a sudden and temporary loss of self-control.

2.2b Objective test

If the jury is satisfied that the defendant did suffer a sudden and temporary loss of self-control, it must then ask whether a reasonable person would have acted in the same way. This limits the defence and ensures that the defendant's response was not completely out of proportion to the provocation.

> Objective tests are concerned with what the ordinary reasonable person would think or do, not what the defendant personally thought or did.

The question naturally arises as to what a 'reasonable person' is and the courts have been asked to consider this issue on many occasions.

***DPP* v *Camplin* (1978)**

The defendant was a 15-year-old boy and the victim was a 50-year-old man who had sexually abused him. The man had abused the defendant and then laughed, at which point the defendant hit and killed him with a chapatti-pan. At the trial, the judge directed the jury to judge the defendant according to the standards of an adult male. The House of Lords held that this was incorrect and maintained that the correct direction was to consider the effect that the provocation would have on a reasonable 15-year-old boy. The question was not would the reasonable adult have acted in the same way but whether the reasonable 15-year-old boy would have done so. The decision meant that the reasonable person was then taken to be an ordinary person with the same powers of self-control as someone of the same age and sex as the defendant and sharing such characteristics as would affect the gravity of the provocation.

Various cases reached the courts on the issue of what characteristics, apart from sex and age, could be attributed to the 'reasonable person'.

***R* v *Smith (Morgan)* (2000)**

The defendant was an alcoholic who also suffered from a depressive illness. After an argument with an old friend, in which the defendant accused his friend of stealing his missing tools, Smith stabbed and killed him. He sought to rely on the victim's denial of stealing the tools as provocation, and the question was whether the 'reasonable person' should be taken to have the same depressive illness, which medical evidence showed lowered his powers of self-control.

The judge in the original trial said that the depressive illness could not be attributed to the reasonable person. The House of Lords instead argued that it was a relevant characteristic and should have been taken into account when deciding the degree of control that society could expect of him. It confirmed that determining relevant characteristics was entirely a matter for the jury.

The judgement in *Smith* was criticised as compromising the objective nature of the test. If the reasonable person is given most of the characteristics of the defendant, the test becomes a subjective one. The criticism intensified after the decision in *Weller*, when it was held that any characteristic of the defendant may be taken into account.

***R* v *Weller* (2004)**
The defendant strangled his 18-year-old girlfriend after an argument about her behaviour regarding other men. The defendant argued that his severe jealousy and possessiveness were relevant characteristics that should be attributed to the reasonable person. The question the jury should ask is whether the reasonable jealous and possessive person would have acted in the same way. After this case, it appeared that any characteristic of the defendant could potentially be taken into account.

Recently, however, there has been a change in attitude by the courts.

***Attorney General for Jersey* v *Holley* (2005)**
The defendant was an alcoholic who killed his girlfriend with an axe while drunk. He did not deny the murder but sought to rely on the partial defence of provocation. The Court of Appeal for Jersey allowed his appeal against his conviction. In order to clarify the law, the Attorney General for Jersey appealed to the Privy Council, which was composed of nine judges from the House of Lords. The majority took the view that *Smith* had been wrongly decided. The reasonable person was an objective standard and the test is whether the defendant showed the powers of self-control to be expected of an ordinary person of the same sex and age. Other characteristics are only relevant to the gravity of the provocation. Thus, since the powers of self-control to be expected of a defendant are now those of the reasonable person, the objective nature of the test has been restored.

***R* v *Mohammed* (2005); *R* v *James* and *R* v *Karimi* (2006)**
The Court of Appeal acknowledged that the decision of the Privy Council in *Holley* was now to be followed rather than the House of Lords decision in *Smith*. As a matter of precedent, the Court of Appeal is bound to follow a decision of the House of Lords rather than a conflicting decision of the Privy Council, but this was acknowledged to be an exceptional case.

Look out for key words in problem questions on provocation such as 'insulted' or 'teased'.

2.3 Cumulative provocation

The requirement that the loss of self-control must be sudden and temporary has caused some to complain that the provocation defence operates in a way that discriminates against women. They claim that provocation is based on the notion of male reactions to violence. When faced with aggression, the traditional male response is to react with violence, but for women, however, this is not often a viable option; for the most part, they will not be able to match the physical strength of a male. When a woman is faced with violence, she may react quite differently and is unlikely to fight back immediately — for example, causing a time delay while she gets a weapon. Despite the difference in reactions, both males and females may experience the requisite loss of self-control.

Make sure that you understand what is meant by cumulative provocation.

In order to combat this apparent sexism, the courts have accepted the idea of 'cumulative provocation', under which previous acts or words may be taken into account when considering whether the defendant was provoked. Cumulative provocation is also sometimes referred to using the phrase 'the straw that broke the camel's back'. The final act or word may not have been serious if considered in isolation, but when added to all of the other provoking acts or words it may have caused the defendant to lose his or her self-control.

The idea of 'slow burn' provocation has been used in domestic violence cases, where women who have suffered years of abuse at the hands of their partners finally 'snap' and kill them. Since they would usually have to wait for an opportunity to attack their partners, provocation was traditionally denied to them as they failed the 'sudden and temporary' loss of control requirement.

***R* v *Thornton (No. 1)* (1992)**
After years of abuse at the hands of her husband, Sara Thornton stabbed him after he called her a 'whore' and said that he would kill her. Her conviction for murder was upheld after the Court of Appeal agreed with the trial judge that her loss of control had not been sudden and temporary. She had gone into the kitchen to get the knife and had sharpened it prior to stabbing him. A second appeal was allowed in 1995 based on the concept of battered-wife syndrome.

***R* v *Ahluwalia* (1992)**
In another domestic violence case, the defendant's husband had abused her for many years. One evening, he threatened her with violence to take place on the next day. He then went to bed and while he was asleep, she poured petrol over him and set it alight. She was charged with murder when he died as a result of his injuries. Her first appeal against conviction failed because the Court of Appeal took into account the delay between the provocation and her response. The court said that while the defendant's reaction had to be sudden, this did not mean that it had to be immediate. However, the longer the delay and the more evidence of deliberation, the more likely that the attack will be viewed as one of revenge rather than provocation. Eventually, Ahluwalia mounted a successful appeal based on the defence of diminished responsibility. It was said in that appeal, however, that a time delay did not automatically mean that the defence of provocation failed, as the defendant might still have had a sudden and temporary loss of control at the last moment.

3 Burden and standard of proof

Once there is some evidence of provocation, the judge must leave the matter to the jury. It is up to the jury to decide whether the defendant was provoked by things said or done or both together, whether the defendant lost his or her self-control as a result, and finally whether a reasonable person of the same age and sex as the defendant but with ordinary powers of self-control would have acted as the defendant did.

4 Effect

If the jury finds that the defendant was provoked, the defendant's liability will be for manslaughter rather than murder.

5 Evaluation

This area has been subject to much examination and debate. The Law Commission recently reviewed this area of the law in its paper 'Partial Defences to Murder' (Consultation Paper No. 173).

The Law Commission concluded that the present law in this area is in need of statutory reform for the following reasons.

5.1 Excuses murder

Some critics argue that it is never justified to kill as a result of any provocation and a sane defendant who kills another unlawfully should always be convicted of murder.

5.2 Scope is too broad

The Law Commission argues that the definition of provocation is too broad, in that it includes behaviour that most people would not describe as provocative. An example can be seen in the case of *Doughty*. The Law Commission argues that it is 'morally offensive' to regard a baby's crying as provocation.

5.3 Scope is too narrow

In some respects, however, the scope of provocation is viewed as too narrow. The requirement that the loss of control be 'sudden and temporary' has worked against defendants — particularly those in abusive relationships.

5.4 Holds the victim responsible for his or her own death

Reliance on the defence of provocation necessitates examination of the victim's actions. Where the victim is the one who has provoked the defendant, focus is placed on the victim's conduct. Many view this as unfair, since deceased victims are unable to respond to any allegations made against them.

5.5 Sexual discrimination

As seen above, the defence of provocation is criticised for its seemingly discriminatory effect. Since it reflects the traditional male response to violence, women have found it difficult to meet the necessary criteria for a successful plea.

6 *Reform*

6.1 Redefine the defence

The Law Commission detailed proposals for a reformed offence in its report 'Partial Defences to Murder'. It recommended that the defence should be available to the defendant if he or she acted in response to:

(a) gross provocation (meaning words or conduct or a combination of words and conduct that caused the defendant to have a justifiable sense of being seriously wronged), **or**

(b) fear of serious violence towards the defendant or another, **or**

(c) a combination of (a) and (b)

Furthermore, it is important that a person of the defendant's age and of ordinary temperament might have reacted in the same or a similar way in the circumstances of the defendant.

The Law Commission further stated that provocation should not apply where it was incited by the defendant for the purpose of providing an excuse to use violence, or the defendant acted in premeditated desire for revenge.

6.2 Merge diminished responsibility and provocation into one defence

The Law Commission considered the possibility of merging diminished responsibility and provocation into one defence, but it did not believe that such a move would solve the current problems.

6.3 Abolish provocation

It has been suggested that the defence of provocation should be abolished, but the Law Commission concluded that this should not be done as long as the mandatory life sentence remains for murder. Currently, there is no indication by the government that the mandatory nature of the sentence in murder cases is to be changed, so it appears that provocation will remain for the foreseeable future.

C Suicide pacts

A suicide pact may occur if two or more parties make an agreement to die. However, if all parties embark upon the pact but one person survives, he or she may be subsequently charged with murder. For example, a husband and wife may agree to commit suicide together. The husband may shoot his wife with the intention of killing her and then shoot himself. If his wife dies but he survives, e.g. he is found and given medical treatment, then he may be charged with his wife's murder. In this case, he would be able to use the defence of suicide pact to reduce his liability to that of manslaughter.

1 *Definition*

Section 4 of the **Homicide Act 1957** provides a defence to a murder charge for the survivor of a suicide pact:

> (1) it shall be manslaughter and shall not be murder for a person acting in pursuance of a suicide pact between himself and another to kill the other or be a party to the other killing himself or being killed by a third party.
>
> (3) for the purposes of this section 'suicide pact' means a common agreement between two or more persons having for its object the death of all of them, whether or not each is to take his own life, but nothing done by a person who enters into a suicide pact shall be treated as done by him in pursuance of the pact unless it is done while he has the settled intention of dying in pursuance of the pact.

2 *Elements*

Like diminished responsibility and provocation, this partial defence only applies to a charge of murder. It must be shown by the defendant that there was a suicide pact in existence and that all parties had the settled intention of dying throughout.

3 Burden and standard of proof

The defendant must prove the existence of the suicide pact on the balance of probabilities.

4 Effect

Like the other defences in this section, if successful the defendant will be convicted of voluntary manslaughter rather than murder and will avoid the mandatory life sentence.

Summary of Topic 3

Diminished responsibility

Definition

Diminished responsibility is defined in s.2 of the **Homicide Act 1957**:

> Where a person kills or is party to a killing of another, he shall not be convicted of murder if he was suffering from such abnormality of mind (whether arising from a condition of arrested or retarded development of mind or any inherent causes or induced by disease or injury) as substantially impaired his mental responsibility for his acts and omissions in doing or being a party to the killing.

Elements

The defendant must be suffering from an abnormality of mind. This must be caused by a condition of arrested or retarded development of mind or any inherent cause or be induced by disease or injury. This covers conditions such as mental deficiency, depression, battered-wife syndrome, premenstrual tension, epilepsy, shock and depression caused by a chemical imbalance in the brain. The abnormality of mind must substantially impair the defendant's mental responsibility for the killing and it is up to the jury to decide whether this was the case. The abnormality does not have to be the only cause of the defendant's actions.

Burden and standard of proof

The defendant must prove, on the balance of probabilities, that he or she was suffering from diminished responsibility at the time of the killing. Medical evidence will be required from at least two experts to substantiate any such claim.

Effect

Diminished responsibility is a special defence that applies only to murder. If pleaded successfully, it acts as a partial defence and will reduce the defendant's liability from murder to that of manslaughter and thus allow him or her to avoid the mandatory life sentence.

Evaluation

The Law Commission recently reviewed the area of voluntary manslaughter in its paper 'Partial Defences to Murder' (Consultation Paper No. 173).

Unclear meaning
It is unclear precisely what 'diminished responsibility' means. 'Abnormality of mind' is simply defined as a state of mind that is 'abnormal'. There are also difficulties in trying to determine whether the defendant's mental responsibility has been 'substantially impaired'.

Burden of proof rests with the defendant
Opponents of the current law say that the burden of proof should be changed so that the onus is on the prosecution.

Defines those in abusive relationships as mentally abnormal
Those in abusive relationships who kill their abusers must claim to be mentally abnormal in order to rely on the defence.

Courts accept defence too easily at times
In some cases involving euthanasia, the courts may take the view that the defendant does not deserve to be labelled a murderer and to face the accompanying life sentence, and so accept a plea of diminished responsibility on the basis of little evidence.

Reform
In its recent review, the Law Commission found that there had been a fall in the successful use of the diminished responsibility defence. However, it stated that the defence appeared to be working and advocated its retention as long as the mandatory life sentence for murder remains.

Provocation

Definition
Provocation is defined in s.3 of the **Homicide Act 1957**:

> Where on a charge of murder there is evidence on which the jury can find that the person charged was provoked (whether by things done or by things said or by both together) to lose his self-control, the question whether the provocation was enough to make a reasonable man do as he did shall be left to be determined by the jury; and in determining that question the jury shall take into account everything both done and said according to the effect which, in their opinion, it would have on a reasonable man.

Elements
Provocation may be caused by things said, things done or both. There is no requirement that such things are illegal. The provocation may come from or be directed at a third party.

There is a subjective and objective element to the defence. The first question that the jury must ask is whether, as a matter of fact, the defendant was provoked to lose his or her self-control. This loss must be 'sudden and temporary'. If so, it must then decide whether a reasonable person would have acted in the same way. The reasonable person is the same age and sex as the defendant and various cases have discussed what other characteristics the reasonable person shares with the defendant. In *Holley* (2005), the Privy Council held that any other characteristics are only relevant to the gravity of the provocation. The powers of self-control to be expected of a defendant are now those of the reasonable person.

Burden and standard of proof

Once there is some evidence of provocation, the judge must leave the matter to the jury. It is up to the jury to decide whether the defendant was provoked by things said or done or both together, whether the defendant lost his or her self-control as a result, and finally whether a reasonable person of the same age and sex as the defendant but with ordinary powers of self-control would have acted as the defendant did.

Effect

Like diminished responsibility, provocation is a special defence that applies only to murder. If pleaded successfully, it acts as a partial defence and will reduce the defendant's liability from murder to that of manslaughter, and thus allow him or her to avoid the mandatory life sentence.

Evaluation

Excuses murder

Critics argue that it is never justified to kill as a result of any provocation and a sane person who kills another unlawfully should be convicted of murder.

Its scope is too broad

Provocation is too broad in that it includes behaviour most people would not accept as provocation, such as a baby crying.

Its scope is too narrow

Provocation is too narrow, as the defendant's loss of control must be 'sudden and temporary', which has worked against defendants — particularly those in abusive relationships.

The victim is held responsible for his or her own death

Where the victim is the person who has provoked the defendant, focus is placed on the victim's conduct. Many view this as unfair, since deceased victims are unable to respond to any allegations made against them.

Sexual discrimination

Provocation reflects the traditional male response to violence, so women have sometimes found it difficult to meet the necessary criteria for a successful plea.

Reform

Redefine the defence

In 'Partial Defences to Murder', the Law Commission recommended that the defence should be available to the defendant if he or she acted in response to:

(a) gross provocation (meaning words or conduct or a combination of words and conduct which caused the defendant to have a justifiable sense of being seriously wronged), **or**

(b) fear of serious violence towards the defendant or another, **or**

(c) a combination of (a) and (b)

Furthermore, it is important that a person of the defendant's age and of ordinary temperament might have reacted in the same or a similar way in the circumstances of the defendant.

The Law Commission further stated that provocation should not apply where it was incited by the defendant for the purpose of providing an excuse to use violence, or the defendant acted in premeditated desire for revenge.

Merge diminished responsibility and provocation into one defence
The Law Commission considered the possibility of merging diminished responsibility and provocation into one defence, but it did not believe that such a move would solve the current problems.

Abolish provocation
It has been suggested that the defence of provocation should be abolished, but the Law Commission concluded that this should not be done as long as the mandatory life sentence for murder remains.

Suicide pacts

A suicide pact may occur if two or more parties make an agreement to die. However, if all parties embark upon the pact but one person survives, he or she may be subsequently charged with murder. The surviving person would be able to use this defence to reduce his or her liability to that of manslaughter. The defendant must prove the existence of the suicide pact on the balance of probabilities. If successful, the defendant will be convicted of voluntary manslaughter and avoid the mandatory life sentence.

TOPIC 4 Involuntary manslaughter

Involuntary manslaughter is a common-law offence.

Involuntary manslaughter has the same *actus reus* as murder (unlawful killing) but a different *mens rea*. Murder requires an intention to kill or to cause grievous bodily harm, whereas involuntary manslaughter does not state what the required *mens rea* is, just that it is something other than intention to kill or to cause grievous bodily harm.

A Constructive manslaughter

Constructive manslaughter is sometimes known as unlawful and dangerous act manslaughter.

This type of involuntary manslaughter requires the defendant to have committed an unlawful and dangerous act. This is the *actus reus* of the crime. The *mens rea* is simply that which is required for the unlawful act.

1 *Unlawful act*

The act must be unlawful. The case of *R* v *Franklin* (1883) stated that the unlawful act must also be a criminal offence rather than a tort (civil wrong).

There have been many drugs cases that have required the courts to assess what an unlawful act is.

***R* v *Cato* (1976)**
Two drug addicts were injecting each other with morphine. The defendant injected his friend, who subsequently died. The unlawful act was administering a noxious substance, defined in s.23 of the **Offences Against the Person Act 1861**. This offence was used because it is not a crime to inject someone. The Court of Appeal upheld the defendant's conviction.

Other unlawful acts include assault (*R* v *Mitchell*, 1983), arson (*R* v *Goodfellow*, 1986) and criminal damage (*R* v *Newbury and Jones*, 1976).

The unlawful act must cause the victim's death. The normal rules of causation apply.

***R* v *Kennedy* (1999)**
The defendant supplied the victim with a syringe of heroin, which the victim injected immediately before leaving. The victim died an hour later. The defendant was charged with constructive manslaughter but he appealed to the Court of Appeal. He argued that it was not the supply of the drug that had caused the death but the victim injecting himself, and, therefore, the self-injection broke the chain of causation. The Court of Appeal upheld the conviction by making the defendant an accomplice to the self-injection.

The case of *R* v *Kennedy* raised many criticisms, as the court did not specify exactly which unlawful act caused the victim's death. The earlier case of *R* v *Dalby* (1982) held that supply of a drug alone could not constitute manslaughter. The Court of Appeal in *R* v *Dias* (2002) quashed the conviction of the defendant in a case that was similar to *Kennedy*. However, in *R* v *Rodgers* (2003) the defendant was found guilty of constructive manslaughter when he helped the victim inject himself by applying a tourniquet.

***R* v *Kennedy* (2005)**
Kennedy got a second appeal to the Court of Appeal in 2005. The Court accepted that mere supply of drugs cannot constitute manslaughter, but it thought that Kennedy was guilty of manslaughter because he did more than merely supply. By making up the syringe of heroin, Kennedy was 'in concert' with the victim, and therefore the unlawful act was administering a noxious substance as defined in s.23 of the **Offences Against the Person Act 1861** (similar to *R* v *Cato*, 1976 above).

2 Dangerous act

The unlawful act must be considered dangerous. The test for dangerousness was established in *R* v *Church* (1967). It is an objective test in that the ordinary reasonable person would see a risk of some harm.

***R* v *Church* (1967)**
The defendant had an argument with a woman in the back of his van. He had been unable to satisfy her sexually and she had slapped him in the face. The defendant knocked her unconscious and, thinking she was dead, he threw her into the river to dispose of the body. She drowned in the river.

The Court of Appeal established the test for dangerousness. The unlawful act must be such as 'all sober and reasonable people would inevitably recognise must subject the other person to, at least, the risk of some harm resulting therefrom, albeit not serious harm.'

As this is an objective test, it did not matter that the defendant did not see a risk of some harm when he threw the victim into the river.

The *Church test* has also been confirmed in *R* v *Ball* (1989).

***R* v *Newbury and Jones* (1976)**
The *Church* test was confirmed in this case, where the House of Lords upheld the conviction of two 15-year-old boys who killed a train guard when they dropped paving stones from a railway bridge onto a passing train.

***R* v *Watson* (1989)**
The defendant burgled the house of an 87-year-old man. The man died of a heart attack shortly afterwards. The court held that the defendant's unlawful act (burglary) became dangerous when he saw that the old man was frail.

This is an example of the 'but for' test for causation.

Watson's conviction was eventually quashed as the court could not prove factual causation — was it the burglary that brought on the heart attack, or was the man going to die anyway?

3 Not an omission

Constructive manslaughter requires that the unlawful act is not an omission.

This type of crime would constitute gross negligence manslaughter (see below).

***R* v *Lowe* (1973)**
A deliberate omission cannot constitute constructive manslaughter. The defendant deliberately neglected a child who died as a result.

4 Mens rea

The defendant does not require any *mens rea* that shows that he or she intended or foresaw a risk of death. Instead, the defendant must have the *mens rea* required for the unlawful and dangerous act.

***R* v *Lamb* (1967)**
The defendant killed his best friend with a revolver. He did not have the appropriate *mens rea*, as neither of the men thought the gun would fire. The defendant was not liable for his friend's death as it was seen as an accident.

The transferred malice rule applies to constructive manslaughter.

***R* v *Mitchell* (1983)**
The defendant had tried to push in nearer the front of a post office queue. An old man tried to stop him and the defendant punched him in the face, causing him to fall back and knock over an 89-year-old woman who subsequently died. The defendant was convicted for the constructive manslaughter of the woman, even though he had no *mens rea* towards her. The court transferred his *mens rea* from the man towards whom he did intend some harm to the woman who died.

B Gross negligence manslaughter

This type of involuntary manslaughter was defined in the case of *R* v *Adomako* (1995). It requires:

- a duty of care
- a breach of that duty that caused death
- a risk of death

The *mens rea* of this crime is described as gross negligence.

Gross negligence manslaughter differs from constructive manslaughter in that:

- it can be committed by omission
- it does not have to be an unlawful act
- there must be a risk of death rather than a risk of some harm

R v *Adomako* (1995)
The defendant was an anaesthetist during the latter part of an eye operation conducted at Mayday Hospital, Croydon on 4 January 1987. Forty-five minutes into the operation, the first anaesthetist and his assistant left to attend another operation. Dr Adomako then became the anaesthetist-in-charge, although his assistant did not arrive until later. The patient died within the next 45 minutes.

An oxygen tube had become disconnected from the ventilator, which the defendant failed to notice for 6 minutes. By this time, the patient had suffered a cardiac arrest and attempts to resuscitate were unsuccessful. There was conflicting evidence as to whether the defendant was actually in the room.

The defendant appealed against his conviction to the Criminal Division of the Court of Appeal, who dismissed the appeal.

This is the leading case for gross negligence manslaughter.

The House of Lords unanimously dismissed a further appeal, upholding the conviction and the sentence. The leading judgement came from the then Lord Chancellor, Lord Mackay of Clashfern, who defined the common-law offence of gross negligence manslaughter and, by overruling *R* v *Seymour* (1983), abolished reckless act manslaughter.

Lord Mackay based the crime of gross negligence manslaughter on the civil rules of negligence.

1 *Duty of care*

A duty of care is established using the civil neighbour principle from *Donoghue* v *Stevenson* (1932). You owe a duty of care to 'persons so closely and directly affected by...my acts or omissions'.

Public policy is where a judge decides a case according to what is best for the interests of the public.

It is a question of law as to whether the defendant owes a duty of care and therefore it is an issue for the judge to decide. Since *Caparo Industries* v *Dickman* (1990), the judge can establish the existence of a duty of care incrementally and does not have to establish one if it is against public policy to do so.

***R* v *Wacker* (2002)**
The defendant tried to smuggle 60 Chinese immigrants into the UK in his lorry. He closed the air vent in order to reduce suspicion. The immigrants suffocated in the back of the lorry and 58 were found dead. The defendant was found guilty of gross negligence manslaughter.

Under the civil law, the defendant would not owe a duty of care because of the principle of *ex turpi causa*. This means that you do not owe a duty of care to people with whom you are carrying out an unlawful activity.

The Court of Appeal stated that the civil principle of *ex turpi causa* did not apply to gross negligence manslaughter, because it would be against public policy for it to do so.

This case was confirmed in *R* v *Willoughby* (2004).

The courts have been reluctant to establish a duty of care in certain circumstances. For example, a pimp did not owe a duty of care to a prostitute to whom he had given heroin, which put her in a coma (*R* v *Khan and Khan*, 1998), nor did a man owe a duty of care to his drunken friend whom he left sleeping in a car and who later died (*Lewin* v *CPS*, 2002).

2 *Breach of duty that caused death*

The breach of duty must have caused death. This means that the rules of causation must also be proved.

In gross negligence manslaughter there must be a breach of duty, which means that the defendant has fallen below the standard of care expected of the ordinary reasonable person. The breach must be serious. It is up to the jury to 'consider whether the extent to which the defendant's conduct departed from the proper standard of care incumbent upon him, involving as it must have done a risk of death to the victim, was such as it should be judged criminal' (Lord MacKay in *R* v *Adomako*, 1995).

***R* v *Becker* (2000)**
A doctor whose patient died from an overdose of the painkillers that he had prescribed was not guilty of gross negligence manslaughter, as he had not fallen below the standard of care expected of the ordinary reasonable doctor.

3 *Risk of death*

***R* v *Singh* (1999)**
A tenant died of carbon monoxide poisoning. It was held that there was a foreseeable risk of death for the landlord to be liable.

'Risk of death' uses an objective test.

In *R* v *Singh* (1999), the trial judge directed the jury that: 'The circumstances must be such that a reasonably prudent person would have foreseen a serious and obvious risk not merely of injury or even serious injury but of death.' This suggests that the 'risk of death' requirement of gross negligence manslaughter is now regarded as an objective test.

The requirement of a risk of death restricts liability. This means that not everyone who owes a duty of care and has breached his or her duty will be convicted of gross negligence manslaughter. There must also be an obvious or foreseen risk of death.

4 Mens rea

Lord MacKay in *R* v *Adomako* (1995) quoted Lord Hewart in an attempt to define the *mens rea* of gross negligence. He did not want to provide a better definition, as he was worried that a jury would not understand it.

***R* v *Bateman* (1925)**
In this case, Lord Hewart CJ said:

This makes the *mens rea* of gross negligence much wider than Cunningham subjective recklessness.

> In order to establish criminal liability, the facts must be such that, in the opinion of the jury, the negligence of the accused went beyond a mere matter of compensation between subjects and showed such disregard for the life and safety of others as to amount to a crime against the state and conduct deserving punishment.

***Attorney General's Reference (No. 2 of 1999)* (2000)**
The physical conduct of the defendant may be enough to prove gross negligence without the need for the jury to consider *mens rea*.

***R* v *Misra and Srivastava* (2004)**
The lack of certainty as to the required *mens rea* (if any) was challenged in this case, where the defence argued that the law of gross negligence manslaughter was in breach of Article 7 of the European Convention on Human Rights. The Court of Appeal rejected this argument, saying that it is a question of fact rather than law for the jury to decide if the defendant's conduct was grossly negligent to the extent that it was criminal.

This case involved the Southall train crash in 1997.

C Reckless manslaughter

There was some confusion after the ruling in *R* v *Adomako* (1995) as to whether reckless manslaughter still existed. In this case, the House of Lords stated that there was no need to have three types of involuntary manslaughter and it abolished objective reckless manslaughter. However, the Court of Appeal in *R* v *Lidar* (1999) allowed the trial judge to let the jury convict using subjective reckless manslaughter.

***R* v *Lidar* (1999)**
The defendant drove off with the victim hanging out of the car window. The victim was killed after falling out of the window and being run over by the defendant.

The Court of Appeal said that there was nothing in the case of *R* v *Adomako* (1995) to suggest that subjective reckless manslaughter had been abolished. It decided that this was not a separate type of involuntary manslaughter, but instead just an aspect of gross negligence manslaughter.

D Evaluation

This area of the law has been subject to much criticism.

The specific nature of the crime of constructive manslaughter means that only cases that are unlawful, dangerous and involve an act rather than an omission will be liable. This means that some cases can 'slip' through, for example if they involve an omission, as in *R* v *Lowe* (1973), or if they do not involve a criminal act, as in *R* v *Franklin* (1883). It is thought that such situations will either fall into the category of gross negligence manslaughter and still result in the defendant being liable, or that it is appropriate for these deaths to be regarded as accidental.

Drugs cases have caused much legal discussion. Cases such as *R* v *Kennedy* (1999) and *R* v *Rodgers* (2003) could be regarded as the courts' attempt to make sure people involved in drugs and drug dealers are found responsible for any resulting death. This could be an example of the courts showing their moral disapproval of such activities and also their way of being strict with such offenders.

The 'dangerous test' for constructive manslaughter from *R* v *Church* (1967) is objective, requiring only a risk of some harm. The 'risk of death' requirement for gross negligence manslaughter is based on an objective test that there was a risk of death (*R* v *Singh*, 1999). This makes the offence of gross negligence manslaughter more difficult to establish than that of constructive manslaughter. The use of objective tests in serious crimes is usually avoided, as the courts feel that it is important only to convict people who see a risk for themselves. It is also unlikely that the jury will not regard a defendant's conduct as dangerous in a case where somebody has died.

The Law Commission Report 1996 did not think it appropriate that a person could be convicted of constructive manslaughter when he or she only had the *mens rea* required for assault. The Home Office Report 2000, however, disagreed with this, as it maintained that a person who commits any illegal violence should be liable for the result of his or her acts, even if he or she did not foresee that the victim would die.

The fact that gross negligence manslaughter is based on civil law has caused much criticism, and the case of *R* v *Misra and Srivastava* (2004) held that the lack of a clearly defined *mens rea* was in breach of the European Convention on Human Rights.

E Reform

A Law Commission report in 1996 recommended that involuntary manslaughter should be abolished and replaced with two new crimes — reckless killing and killing by gross carelessness.

The government's Home Office Report 2000 agreed with this proposal, in that reckless killing would be based on subjective recklessness, and killing by gross carelessness would not require a breach of duty of care. The government has since decided not to go ahead with these proposals.

Summary of Topic 4

Involuntary manslaughter has the same *actus reus* as murder (unlawful killing) but a different *mens rea*.

Constructive manslaughter

Unlawful act

The act must be unlawful. The case of *R* v *Franklin* (1883) stated that the unlawful act must also be a criminal offence rather than a tort (civil wrong). There have been many drugs cases, which have required the courts to assess what is an unlawful act (*R* v *Cato*, 1976). The unlawful act must cause the victim's death. The normal rules of causation apply (*R* v *Kennedy*, 1999).

Dangerous act

The unlawful act must be considered dangerous. The test for dangerousness was established in *R* v *Church* (1967). It is an objective test in that the ordinary reasonable person would see a risk of some harm.

Not an omission

Constructive manslaughter requires that there must be an unlawful act, and an omission will not suffice (*R* v *Lowe*, 1973).

Mens rea

The defendant does not require any *mens rea* that shows he or she intended or foresaw a risk of death. Instead, the defendant must have the *mens rea* required for the unlawful and dangerous act (*R* v *Lamb*, 1967). The transferred malice rule applies to constructive manslaughter (*R* v *Mitchell*, 1983).

Gross negligence manslaughter

This type of involuntary manslaughter was defined in the case of *R* v *Adomako* (1995).

Duty of care

A duty of care is established using the civil neighbour principle from *Donoghue* v *Stevenson* (1932). You owe a duty of care to 'persons so closely and directly affected by...my acts or omissions'.

It is a question of law as to whether the defendant owes a duty of care and therefore it is an issue for the judge to decide. Since *Caparo Industries* v *Dickman* (1990), the judge can establish the existence of a duty of care incrementally and does not have to establish one if it is against public policy to do so, e.g. *R* v *Wacker* (2002).

The courts have been reluctant to establish a duty of care in certain circumstances. For example, a pimp did not owe a duty of care to a prostitute to whom he had given heroin, which put her in a coma (*R* v *Khan and Khan*, 1998).

Breach of duty caused death

There must also be a breach of duty, which means that the defendant has fallen below the standard of care expected of the ordinary reasonable person. The breach must be serious. It is up to the jury to 'consider whether the extent to which the defendant's conduct departed from the proper standard of care incumbent upon him, involving as it must have done a risk of death to the victim, was such as it should be judged criminal' (Lord MacKay in *R* v *Adomako*, 1995), e.g. *R* v *Becker* (2000).

Risk of death

In *R* v *Singh* (1999), the trial judge directed the jury that: 'The circumstances must be such that a reasonably prudent person would have foreseen a serious and obvious risk not merely of injury or even serious injury but of death.'

Mens rea

Lord MacKay in *R* v *Adomako* (1995) quoted Lord Hewart in an attempt to define the *mens rea* of gross negligence. He did not want to provide a better definition, as he was worried that a jury would not understand it.

It was stated in *R* v *Bateman* (1925):

> In order to establish criminal liability, the facts must be such that, in the opinion of the jury, the negligence of the accused went beyond a mere matter of compensation between subjects and showed such disregard for the life and safety of others as to amount to a crime against the state and conduct deserving punishment.

The lack of certainty as to the required *mens rea* (if any) was challenged in the case of *R* v *Misra and Srivastava*, 2004), where the defence argued that the law of gross negligence manslaughter was in breach of Article 7 of the European Convention on Human Rights.

Reckless manslaughter

The House of Lords in *R* v *Adomako* (1995) stated that there was no need to have three types of involuntary manslaughter and it abolished objective reckless manslaughter. However, the Court of Appeal in *R* v *Lidar* (1999) allowed the trial judge to let the jury convict using subjective reckless manslaughter. It decided that this was not a separate type of involuntary manslaughter, but instead just an aspect of gross negligence manslaughter.

Evaluation

The specific nature of the crime of constructive manslaughter means that only cases that are unlawful, dangerous and involve an act rather than an omission will be liable.

Drugs cases have caused a lot of legal discussion, e.g. *R* v *Kennedy* (1999) and *R* v *Rodgers* (2003).

The 'dangerous test' for constructive manslaughter from *R* v *Church* (1967) is objective, requiring only a risk of some harm. The 'risk of death' requirement for gross negligence manslaughter is based on an objective test that there was a risk of death (*R* v *Singh*, 1999). This makes the offence of gross negligence manslaughter more difficult to establish than the 'dangerous test' for constructive manslaughter.

The Law Commission Report 1996 did not think it appropriate that a person could be convicted of constructive manslaughter when he or she only had the *mens rea* required for assault. The Home Office Report 2000 disagreed with this, as it maintained that a person who commits any illegal violence should be liable for the result of his or her acts, even if he or she did not foresee that the victim would die.

The fact that gross negligence manslaughter is based on civil law has caused much criticism.

Reform

A Law Commission report in 1996 recommended that involuntary manslaughter should be abolished and replaced with two new crimes — reckless killing and killing by gross carelessness.

TOPIC 5 Non-fatal offences

Non-fatal offences against the person vary in seriousness of the injury to the victim and according to the *mens rea* held by the defendant. Assault and battery are often committed at the same time and are known as common assault. Actual bodily harm and the two types of grievous bodily harm are defined in the **Offences Against the Person Act 1861**.

A Assault

Common law is law made by judges.

Section 39 of the **Criminal Justice Act 1988** provides that assault is a summary offence with a maximum sentence on conviction of 6 months' imprisonment or a fine. Assault is not defined in an Act of Parliament, as it is a common-law offence.

***R* v *Venna* (1976)**
This case provided the accepted definition of assault as 'the intentional or reckless causing of an apprehension of immediate unlawful personal violence'.

1 Actus reus

Actus reus means 'guilty act'.

The *actus reus* of assault is any act that makes the victim fear that unlawful force is about to be used against him or her. No force need actually be applied, and actions such as raising a fist, pointing a gun or brandishing a sword will be sufficient. The word 'fear' has been interpreted to mean 'apprehend'.

For many years the courts have debated whether words can amount to an assault. In *R* v *Meade and Belt* (1823), people were gathered around a house and started to sing menacing songs and to use violent language. Judge Holroyd said that 'no words or singing are equivalent to an assault'. However in *R* v *Wilson* (1955), Lord Goddard stated of the accused: 'He called out "Get out the knives", which itself would be an assault.' As *Wilson* is a more recent case, this outcome is preferred.

Words or silence can be an assault.

More recently, the House of Lords decided that a silent telephone call can constitute an assault. If the psychological injury caused is significant, this could even constitute ABH or GBH (*R* v *Ireland*, *R* v *Burstow*, 1997).

There is no assault if it is obvious to the victim that the defendant cannot or will not carry out his or her threat of violence.

***Tuberville* v *Savage* (1669)**
Annoyed by someone's comments to him, the defendant put his hand on his sword, which by itself would have been enough to constitute an assault. However, at the same time he said: 'If it were not assize time I would not take such language.' This meant that since judges were hearing criminal cases in town at the time, he had no intention of using violence. His statement negated the threat.

The courts have given a fairly generous interpretation of the concept of immediacy.

The victim must fear *immediate* threat of harm, not at some time in the future.

***Smith* v *Chief Superintendent, Woking Police Station* (1983)**
The victim was at home in her ground-floor flat dressed in her nightdress. She was terrified when she suddenly saw the defendant standing in her garden staring at

her through the window. The court held he was liable for assault, on the grounds that the victim feared immediate infliction of force, even though she was safely locked inside the building.

2 Mens rea

Mens rea means 'guilty mind'.

The *mens rea* of assault is either intention or Cunningham recklessness. The defendant must have either intended to cause the victim to fear the infliction of immediate and unlawful force, or must have seen the risk that such fear would be created.

B Battery

Section 39 of the **Criminal Justice Act 1988** provides that battery is a summary offence, punishable by up to 6 months' imprisonment or a fine. It is also a common-law offence.

1 Actus reus

The *actus reus* of battery consists of the application of unlawful force on another. Any unlawful physical contact can amount to a battery. There is no need to prove harm or pain — a mere touch can be sufficient.

Battery can be direct or indirect. Direct battery is force applied directly by one person to another, e.g. a slap or a punch. Indirect battery is applied using an implement or vehicle.

These two cases are examples of indirect battery.

***Fagan* v *Metropolitan Police Commissioner* (1969)**
The defendant drove onto the foot of a police officer and was guilty of battery.

***Haystead* v *DPP* (2000)**
The defendant punched a woman twice in the face while she was holding her baby. As a result, she dropped the baby and he hit his head on the floor. The defendant was found guilty of a battery against the baby, as he had indirectly applied force.

To constitute a battery, the victim need not be aware that he or she is about to be struck. Therefore, if someone is struck from behind this will still constitute battery, and he or she need not have seen it coming.

It is settled law that there can be a battery where there has been no direct contact with the victim's body — touching his or her clothing may be enough to constitute this offence.

***R* v *Thomas* (1985)**
The judge stated that touching a woman's skirt was equivalent to touching the woman herself.

An omission can amount to the *actus reus* of battery.

***R* v *Santana-Bermudez* (2003)**
The defendant omitted to give warning that he had a hypodermic needle in his pocket during a police search. A police woman was struck by the needle, which caused bleeding. This was held to constitute a battery.

2 Mens rea

The *mens rea* of battery is intention or Cunningham recklessness, i.e. intention or recklessness as to the application of unlawful force.

Often the offences of assault and battery occur at the same time. This is known as common assault. The police and Crown Prosecution Service have agreed the Joint Charging Standards, which set out the types of injury that will be regarded as common assault. Such injuries include:
- minor bruising
- grazing
- small cuts
- swelling

C Actual bodily harm (Section 47)

1 *Definition*

Actual bodily harm and grievous bodily harm are defined in the **Offences Against the Person Act 1861**.

Section 47 of the **Offences Against the Person Act 1861** states that it is an offence to commit 'any assault occasioning actual bodily harm'. The offence is triable either way and carries a maximum sentence of 5 years' imprisonment.

2 Actus reus

ABH is defined in *R* v *Chan-Fook* (1994).

The *actus reus* of actual bodily harm (ABH) has been interpreted as assault or battery that causes 'actual bodily harm'. This has been given the wide definition of 'any hurt or injury calculated to interfere with the health or comfort of the victim' (*R* v *Miller*, 1954). ABH can therefore occur where discomfort to the person is caused. However, in *R* v *Chan-Fook* (1994), Lord Justice Hobhouse said in the Court of Appeal that 'the word "actual" indicates that the injury (although there is no need for it to be permanent) should not be so trivial as to be wholly insignificant'.

ABH can include psychiatric injury and nervous shock, but not mere emotions such as fear, distress or panic. The injury must be an identifiable clinical condition (*R* v *Ireland*, *R* v *Burstow*, 1997).

3 Mens rea

The *mens rea* for ABH is the same as for assault and battery. No additional *mens rea* is required.

***R* v *Roberts* (1978)**

Late at night, the defendant gave a girl a lift in his car. During the journey he began to make sexual advances, touching the girl's clothes. Frightened that he was going to rape her, she jumped out of the moving car, injuring herself. It was held that the defendant had committed the *actus reus* of a s.47 offence by touching the girls clothing (battery) and this act had caused her to suffer ABH. The defendant argued that he neither intended to cause her ABH, nor had seen any risk of her suffering ABH as a result of his advances. This argument was rejected; the court held that the *mens rea* for battery was sufficient in itself and there was no need for any extra *mens rea* regarding ABH.

The decision in *R* v *Roberts* was confirmed in *R* v *Savage* (1991).

***R* v *Savage* (1991)**

The defendant went to a local pub, where she spotted her husband's new girlfriend at a table, having a drink with some friends. She went up to the table, intending to throw a pint of beer over the girlfriend. On reaching the table she said 'Nice to meet you, darling' and threw the beer, but as she did so, she accidentally let go of the glass as well, which broke and cut the girl's wrist. The defendant argued that she lacked sufficient *mens rea* to be liable for a s.47 offence because her intention had only been to throw the beer and she had not seen the risk that the glass might injure the girlfriend. This argument was rejected because the defendant intended to apply unlawful force (the *mens rea* for battery) and there was no need to prove that she intended to cause ABH, or that she was reckless in causing it.

The police and Crown Prosecution Service have agreed the Joint Charging Standards, which set out the types of injury that will be regarded as ABH. Such injuries include:

- minor fractures (such as a broken nose)
- severe bruising
- loss of consciousness
- small cuts that require stitches
- psychiatric injury

D Grievous bodily harm (Section 20)

1 Definition

The difference between s.20 GBH and s.47 ABH is one of degree, with grievous bodily harm being a much more serious offence.

According to s.20 of the **Offences Against the Person Act 1861**:

> Whosoever shall unlawfully and maliciously wound or inflict any grievous bodily harm upon any other person either with or without any weapon or instrument shall be guilty of an offence triable either way and being convicted thereof shall be liable to imprisonment for 5 years.

2 Actus reus

GBH is defined in *DPP* v *Smith* (1961).

The *actus reus* of the s.20 offence is unlawfully and maliciously wounding or inflicting grievous bodily harm (GBH). In *DPP* v *Smith* (1961), the House of Lords emphasised that GBH should be given its ordinary meaning, i.e. 'really serious harm'. This was confirmed in *R* v *Saunders* (1985), where the Court of Appeal said there is no real difference between the meaning of 'serious' and 'really serious'.

The word 'inflict' has been interpreted to mean that the grievous bodily harm must be caused by the direct application of force, e.g. hitting, kicking or stabbing, but not digging a hole for the victim to fall into, for example. However, in practice the courts have given a fairly wide interpretation as to when force is direct.

***R* v *Martin* (1881)**
While a play was being performed at a theatre, the defendant placed an iron bar across the exit, turned off the staircase lights and shouted 'Fire!' The audience panicked and in the rush to escape people were seriously injured. The defendant was found liable under s.20, even though strictly speaking it is difficult to view the application of force as truly direct.

***R* v *Halliday* (1896)**
This is another wide interpretation of the word 'inflict'. The defendant's behaviour frightened his wife so much that she jumped out of the bedroom window to get away from him. The injuries she suffered as a result of the fall were found to have been directly applied, so that the defendant could be liable under s.20.

***R* v *Dica* (2004)**
The Court of Appeal held that a person could be liable for s.20 GBH by infecting another person with AIDS.

A 'wound' requires a break in the first two layers of skin, so there is normally bleeding, though a graze is sufficient.

***C* v *Eisenhower* (1984)**
The defendant fired an air pistol, hitting the victim in the eye with a pellet. This ruptured a blood vessel in the eye, causing internal bleeding, but this was not sufficient to constitute 'wounding' as the skin had not been broken.

3 Mens rea

The *mens rea* of s.20 GBH is described by the word 'maliciously'. In *R* v *Cunningham* (1957), it was stated that for the purposes of the 1861 Act, 'maliciously' meant 'intentionally or recklessly'.

There is no need to intend GBH or wounding, or to be reckless as to whether GBH or wounding might be caused. The defendant needs only to intend or be reckless that his or her actions could cause some physical damage.

***R* v *Grimshaw* (1984)**
The defendant was in a pub when she heard someone insult her boyfriend. She turned round and struck the person, pushing the glass he was holding in his face

and causing considerable injury. She was found guilty under s.20. She had inflicted grievous bodily harm and she had the relevant *mens rea*, having at least foreseen that the victim would suffer some harm. Therefore, if a defendant realises that some slight injury might be caused as a result of his or her actions, that realisation makes him or her guilty under s.20.

***R* v *Parmenter* (1991)**
The defendant threw a baby into the air and caught it, causing GBH. The defendant said he had done this before with slightly older children and was unaware that his actions were likely to cause harm to a young baby. The judge held that the defendant was not guilty as he did not intend to injure the child, nor did he realise there was a risk of injury to the child.

The police and the Crown Prosecution Service have agreed the Joint Charging Standards, which set out the types of injury that will be regarded as GBH. Such injuries include:

- serious injuries
- broken bones
- dislocated joints
- injury causing permanent disability or disfigurement

E Grievous bodily harm (Section 18)

1 *Definition*

Section 18 of the **Offences Against the Person Act 1861** states that:

> Whosoever shall unlawfully and maliciously by any means whatsoever wound or cause any grievous bodily harm to any person, with intent to do some grievous bodily harm to any person, or with intent to resist or prevent the lawful apprehension or detainer of any person, shall be guilty of an offence triable only on indictment, and being convicted thereof shall be liable to imprisonment for life.

2 Actus reus

The *actus reus* for s.18 is similar to s.20 and requires proof of either GBH or wounding. The *actus reus* of wounding and the *actus reus* of GBH have the same meaning as under s.20.

3 Mens rea

To satisfy the *mens rea*, the prosecution must prove intention to cause GBH or intention to avoid arrest. The crucial difference between s.20 and s.18 GBH is in the *mens rea*; while recklessness can be sufficient for s.20, intention is always required for s.18.

F Evaluation

Lord Justice Henry said in *R* v *Lynsey* (1995): 'Bad laws cost money and clog up courts with better things to do.'

The non-fatal offences have been subject to much criticism over the years:

- The wording of the statutory defences is inconsistent and old-fashioned.
- Assault and battery are still common-law offences.
- The sentencing of the offences is inconsistent.

1 *Wording*

Many of the words used to define non-fatal offences have been criticised as being out of date and ambiguous.

1.1 Assault

The word 'assault' has adopted a different meaning over the years. It is commonly used to explain a situation where someone has been hurt. The use of the term 'serious assault' refers to grievous bodily harm, rather than fear of unlawful force as it legally means.

1.2 Fear

An assault requires that the victim be in fear of unlawful force. 'Be in fear' has since been changed to the more suitable term 'apprehend'. This is because there is a difference between someone being frightened that he or she is going to be hit and someone apprehending that he or she is going to be hit.

A common example here would be when a man is assaulted by a woman.

1.3 Battery

Battery only requires the slightest touch by the defendant. However, the modern use of the word suggests that there is a much greater level of harm.

1.4 Cause

There is inconsistency in the words used in the **Offences Against the Person Act 1861** because it is a consolidating Act, meaning that it is made up of much older Acts of Parliament that have been brought together. Section 18 uses the words 'to cause' GBH, s.20 uses the words 'to inflict' GBH and s.47 uses the words 'to occasion' ABH. All of these words have required the court to interpret them as meaning 'cause'. Such unnecessary interpretation could be avoided if Parliament were to redraft the 1861 Act.

1.5 Wound

The definition of a wound as a break in the first two layers of skin means that, in theory, the slightest cut that bleeds would constitute GBH. In practice, the courts accept that a small cut could be ABH or even battery.

1.6 ABH and GBH

The terms 'actual bodily harm' and 'grievous bodily harm' are not commonly used in modern English.

1.7 Resist arrest

The inclusion of 'resisting arrest' in the definition of s.18 GBH is confusing, as it allows a defendant to be charged with GBH when he or she has *only* resisted arrest.

1.8 Maliciously

While this word is used to define the *mens rea* of some of the offences, there is no need to show any malice. This word is no longer used in legal terminology.

2 *Sentencing*

The statutory guidelines appropriate sentences for the offences are confusing.

2.1 Assault and battery

Assault and battery are summary offences that are punishable by 6 months' imprisonment. The advantage of this sentence is that such cases can be dealt with at the Magistrates' Court, and the expense of a Crown Court trial is avoided. This saves the courts time and money, since the majority of non-fatal offences are either assault or battery.

2.2 ABH and s.20 GBH

Both ABH and s.20 GBH carry the same sentencing guideline of 5 years' imprisonment. It seems unnecessary to have two offences that have the same penalty, even though GBH is supposed to be much more serious than ABH.

2.3 Section 18 GBH

Section 18 GBH carries a penalty of anything up to life imprisonment, because the *mens rea* of this offence is considered much more serious than s.20 GBH. If the victim had died, the defendant would have been charged with murder.

The criticism is that the two types of GBH have extremely different sentences. Section 20 gets 5 years' imprisonment, whereas s.18 affords anything up to life imprisonment. The reason for this difference is due to the defendant's *mens rea*. There is no recognition of the fact that the victim could be just as seriously hurt in both instances.

3 *Inconsistency*

3.1 Charge

It is quite common for a person to be charged with a lesser offence than the one he or she has actually committed to cut costs. For example, a person who has committed GBH may be charged with ABH, which can be tried at the Magistrates' Court. This will save the court time and money, as a charge of GBH would require an expensive Crown Court trial.

In addition, it makes no difference whether a person is charged with s.20 GBH or s.47 ABH, as both offences are punishable by a sentence of up to 5 years' imprisonment.

3.2 Plea bargaining

The prosecution may charge the defendant with a lesser offence if he or she agrees to a guilty plea. This is known as plea bargaining. It saves the court time and money, as it is not necessary to hold a trial. The defendant will be given a more lenient sentence for an early guilty plea.

3.3 Common law

Since assault and battery are frequent offences, it would seem more appropriate for their definitions to be codified in an Act of Parliament.

G Reform

1 *Law Commission Report 1993*

In 1993, the Law Commission produced a report entitled 'Offences Against the Person and General Principles'. This report redrafted the non-fatal offences and criticised the current offences. The three main criticisms of the current law were for its:

- complicated, obscure and old-fashioned language
- complicated and technical structure
- complete unintelligibility to the layman

The Law Commission also produced the Draft Criminal Law Bill, which redefined the offences. The recommendations of this report have never been adopted.

2 *Home Office Report 1998*

You can view this bill on the Home Office website: www.homeoffice.gov.uk

The Labour government produced the Draft Offences Against the Person Bill 1998 following the Home Office report 'Violence: Reforming the Offences Against the Person Act 1861'.

2.1 The new offences

- clause 1: intentional serious injury
- clause 2: reckless serious injury
- clause 3: intentional or reckless injury
- clause 4: assault

2.2 The new sentences

The sentences have stayed the same, with the exception of clause 2. This replaces s.20 GBH, which used to carry a punishment of 5 years' imprisonment. The new clause 2 would increase this to 7 years' imprisonment. Sentences proposed are as follows:

- intentional serious injury: life
- reckless serious injury: 7 years

- intentional or reckless injury: 5 years
- assault: 6 months

2.3 Other changes

- Clauses 1 and 2 will only include wounds that are considered by the court to be 'serious injury'.
- Clause 1 is the only offence that can be committed by omission.
- Intentional serious injury caused by disease would be allowed as a clause 1 offence. However, reckless serious injury caused by disease (clause 2) would not be allowed. This would change the current law established in *R* v *Dica* (2004).
- The *mens rea* of recklessness used in both clause 2 and clause 3 would require proof that the defendant saw a risk of the injury that he or she actually caused. This changes the current law that recklessness only requires the defendant to foresee some harm (*R* v *Roberts*, *R* v *Savage* and *R* v *Grimshaw*).

Summary of Topic 5

Assault

Section 39 of the **Criminal Justice Act 1988** provides that assault is a summary offence with a maximum sentence on conviction of 6 months' imprisonment or a fine. Assault is not defined in an Act of Parliament, as it is a common-law offence.

Actus reus

The *actus reus* of assault is any act that makes the victim fear that unlawful force is about to be used against him or her. The word 'fear' has been interpreted to mean 'apprehend'. Words can be an assault (*R* v *Wilson*, 1955), as can silent phone calls (*R* v *Ireland*, *R* v *Burstow*, 1997). There is no assault if it is obvious to the victim that the defendant cannot or will not carry out his or her threat of violence (*Tuberville* v *Savage*, 1669). The victim must fear immediate threat of harm (*Smith* v *Chief Superintendent, Woking Police Station*, 1983).

Mens rea

The *mens rea* of assault is either intention or Cunningham recklessness.

Battery

Section 39 of the **Criminal Justice Act 1988** provides that battery is a summary offence, punishable by up to 6 months' imprisonment or a fine. It is also a common-law offence.

Actus reus

The *actus reus* of battery consists of the application of unlawful force on another. Any unlawful physical contact can amount to battery. There is no need to prove harm or pain — a mere touch can be sufficient (*R* v *Thomas*, 1985) — and it can be indirect (*Fagan* v *Metropolitan Police Commissioner*, 1969).

Mens rea

The *mens rea* of battery is intention or Cunningham recklessness, i.e. intention or recklessness as to the application of unlawful force.

'Either way' means a case can be heard in the Magistrates' Court or the Crown Court.

Actual bodily harm (Section 47)

Section 47 of the **Offences Against the Person Act 1861** states that it is an offence to commit 'any assault occasioning actual bodily harm'. The offence is triable either way and carries a maximum sentence of 5 years' imprisonment.

Actus reus

The *actus reus* of ABH has been interpreted as assault or battery that causes 'actual bodily harm'. In *R* v *Chan-Fook* (1994), Lord Justice Hobhouse said in the Court of Appeal that 'the word "actual" indicates that the injury (although there is no need for it to be permanent) should not be so trivial as to be wholly insignificant'. ABH can include psychiatric injury and nervous shock, but not mere emotions such as fear, distress or panic (*R* v *Ireland*, *R* v *Burstow*, 1997).

Mens rea

The *mens rea* for ABH is the same as for assault and battery. No additional *mens rea* is required (*R* v *Roberts*, 1978 and *R* v *Savage*, 1991).

Grievous bodily harm (Section 20)

According to s.20 of the **Offences Against the Person Act 1861**:

> Whosoever shall unlawfully and maliciously wound or inflict any grievous bodily harm upon any other person either with or without any weapon or instrument shall be guilty of an offence triable either way and being convicted thereof shall be liable to imprisonment for 5 years.

Actus reus

The *actus reus* of the s.20 offence is unlawfully and maliciously wounding or inflicting grievous bodily harm. In *DPP* v *Smith* (1961), the House of Lords emphasised that GBH should be given its ordinary meaning, i.e. 'really serious harm'. The word 'inflict' has been given a wide interpretation (*R* v *Martin*, 1881). A 'wound' requires a break in the skin, so there is normally bleeding, though a graze is sufficient (*C* v *Eisenhower*, 1984).

Mens rea

The *mens rea* of s.20 GBH is described by the word 'maliciously'. In *R* v *Cunningham* (1957), it was stated that for purposes of the 1861 Act, 'maliciously' meant 'intentionally or recklessly', and reckless is used in the subjective Cunningham sense. There is no need to intend GBH or wounding, or to be reckless as to whether GBH or wounding might be caused. The defendant needs only to intend or be reckless that his or her actions could cause some physical damage (*R* v *Grimshaw*, 1984).

Grievous bodily harm (Section 18)

Section 18 of the **Offences Against the Person Act 1861** states that:

> Whosoever shall unlawfully and maliciously by any means whatsoever wound or cause any grievous bodily harm to any person, with intent to do some grievous bodily harm to any person, or with intent to resist or prevent the lawful apprehension or detainer of any person, shall be guilty of an offence triable only on indictment, and being convicted thereof shall be liable to imprisonment for life.

Actus reus

This is the same as s.20 GBH.

Mens rea

The *mens rea* of an s.18 offence is the intention to cause GBH.

Evaluation

The non-fatal offences have been subject to much criticism over the years. The wording of the statutory defences is inconsistent and old-fashioned, assault and battery are still common-law offences and the sentencing of the offences is inconsistent.

Reform

In 1993, the Law Commission produced a report that redrafted the non-fatal offences and criticised the current offences. However, the recommendations of this report have never been adopted.

The Labour government produced the Draft Offences Against the Person Bill 1998, which created new offences:

- clause 1: intentional serious injury
- clause 2: reckless serious injury
- clause 3: intentional or reckless injury
- clause 4: assault

TOPIC 6 Consent

On some occasions, the consent of the victim may operate to prevent the defendant from incurring liability for what would otherwise be an offence.

A Definition

The general rule is that no liability is incurred if a person inflicts minor harm with the consent of the victim. Consent operates as a defence because the courts recognise that individuals have autonomy over their own lives. However, there are limits as to what a person may consent to, and while consent may be available as a defence to non-fatal and sexual offences, it is not available for charges of murder or manslaughter, as no one may consent to his or her own death at the hands of another.

***Pretty* v *UK* (2002)**
Diane Pretty suffered from terminal motor neurone disease. She wished to end her life but was physically incapable of committing suicide. She wanted a guarantee from the Director of Public Prosecutions that her husband would not be prosecuted for assisting in her suicide since she had consented to this. The DPP refused to grant such immunity. Diane Pretty appealed to the European Court of Human Rights but was unsuccessful. Euthanasia remains a crime in the UK.

B Elements

1 Consent must be valid

The victim's consent to the harm will only be valid if the victim understands the nature of the act and knows exactly to what he or she is consenting. The victim must have the capacity to consent — children and those suffering from mental illness are not able to give valid consent.

***Burrell* v *Harmer* (1967)**
The defendant was charged with ABH after he tattooed two children aged 12 and 13. Their consent was held to be invalid as they had not understood the nature of the act, specifically that pain would be involved.

Following *Gillick* v *West Norfolk and Wisbech AHA* (1986), parents may give consent on behalf of their child until the child has sufficient understanding of what is proposed. This is sometime termed 'Gillick competence'.

2 Consent must be informed

***R* v *Dica* (2004)**
The defendant slept with two women who were unaware that he was HIV positive. Under the old case of *Clarence* (1888), by consenting to sexual intercourse the

victims would also have been consenting to the risk of injury or illness incidental to it. The Court of Appeal in *Dica* held that this was no longer the case. The defendants had not consented to the risk of HIV infection, as they had been unaware that the defendant was infected. This notion of informed consent was followed in *Konzani* (2005) — another case of HIV infection. The defendant could not rely on the defence of consent, as his victims had only consented to unprotected sex and not to the risk of infection with a fatal disease.

3 Consent by fraud

If the defendant has obtained the victim's consent by fraudulent means, this will not always render the consent invalid. Fraud will only invalidate consent if the victim is deceived as to the identity of the defendant or the nature and quality of his or her act.

***R* v *Richardson* (1998)**
The defendant was a dentist who had continued to practise despite being 'struck off' by the General Dental Council. She was convicted of ABH but this was overturned on appeal. The Court of Appeal held that the patients had consented to be treated by her. They were aware of her identity and the nature and quality of the act that she was performing. It was not relevant that they would have refused consent had they known that she had been suspended.

***R* v *Tabassum* (2000)**
The defendant pretended that he was carrying out a medical examination and examined the breasts of three women. He also told them that he had medical qualifications, but this was untrue too. His convictions for indecent assault were upheld on appeal, as he had deceived the women as to the nature and quality of his act.

4 Limitations on consent

In problem questions, consider the level of injury that has been inflicted. Consent will be a defence to common assault, but must fall into one of the exceptions for anything more serious.

Generally, a victim may consent to assault or battery. In *Collins and Wilcock* (1984), it was stated that people are also taken to consent implicitly to the 'physical contacts of ordinary life'. Thus, people who travel on a train during rush hour or who visit the shops during the busy Christmas period cannot take action against those who bump into or jostle them.

Limitations are placed on the defence, however. If the defendant has inflicted injury amounting to ABH or worse, the defence of consent will not be allowed, unless the activity falls into the category of exceptions.

5 Exceptions

Certain activities inevitably mean that the victim will sustain injury beyond assault or battery. A defendant may still be able to rely on the operation of consent, however, provided that the activity is deemed to fall into a category of recognised exceptions. Such exceptions include, but are not limited to, surgery, tattooing and piercing, sports, horseplay and sexual acts.

5.1 Surgery

Many types of surgery require that a wound be inflicted in order to facilitate an operation. The patient is allowed to consent to this level of injury, as the surgery is being carried out for his or her benefit.

5.2 Tattooing and piercing

Adults are able to consent to tattoos and piercing. This was also extended to branding following the case of *Wilson* (see below).

5.3 Sports

Since sports are deemed to be socially beneficial, participants are able to consent to injuries sustained during the course of a game.

The courts will draw a distinction between injuries during the course of the game and off-the-ball incidents.

***R* v *Billinghurst* (1978)**
The defendant punched an opponent and fractured his jaw in an off-the-ball incident during a rugby match. The defendant tried to rely on the victim's consent, arguing that rugby is a game involving physical contact, to which the players are taken to consent. However, the jury convicted him of GBH after deciding that he had gone beyond what was being consented to.

***R* v *Barnes* (2004)**
The defendant injured another player during a football match. He was charged with GBH and sought to rely on the victim's consent to the risk of force inherent in the game. His conviction was overturned on appeal. The Court of Appeal gave guidance on the factors taken into consideration when determining whether criminal liability should arise following injuries sustained during sports. Such factors include the surrounding circumstances, e.g. the level at which the game was being played, the type of sport, the amount of force used and the defendant's state of mind.

5.4 Horseplay

The courts have accepted consent as a defence even to serious injury sustained during horseplay. It is thought that this is because it is an area in which the courts do not want to see criminal prosecutions.

***R* v *Jones* (1986)**
The victim was thrown into the air by his classmates. He sustained a broken arm and a ruptured spleen. Despite the serious nature of his injuries, the defence of consent was allowed as the boys involved, including the victim, had treated the incident as a joke and there was no intention to cause injury.

***R* v *Aiken* (1992)**
The victim suffered serious burns after an RAF initiation ceremony. The defendant was able to rely on the defence of consent as the victim had willingly participated. He was acquitted of GBH.

5.5 Sexual acts

***R* v *Brown and Others* (1993)**
The defendants were members of a group that engaged in sadomasochistic homosexual activities, including genital torture and branding. The acts were done

in private, with the consent of everyone involved. The police found videos of the activities and the men were charged with various counts of both ABH and GBH. The question arose as to whether the defendants could rely on the consent of the victims as a defence. The majority of the House of Lords decided that such activities were not conducive to the welfare of society and so declined to include them in the list of recognised exceptions to the rule that a victim cannot consent to anything beyond common assault. The convictions were upheld.

A similar situation arose in the case of *Wilson* but the courts took a different view.

***R* v *Wilson* (1996)**
The defendant used hot knives to brand his initials onto his wife's bottom at her request. Her injuries were reported to the police by her doctor and the defendant was charged with ABH. His conviction was overturned on appeal. The Court of Appeal held that the act was no more dangerous than tattooing and thus the defence of consent was available.

***R* v *Slingsby* (1995)**
The defendant and the victim met at a nightclub. They engaged in various consensual sexual activities, during which the defendant's ring caused internal cuts to his victim. Neither the defendant nor his victim realised this. The victim's injuries later became infected and she died of septicaemia. The defendant was charged with manslaughter. However, he was acquitted, as the acts had been undertaken with the consent of the victim and he had not intended to cause injury, thereby lacking the relevant *mens rea*.

C Burden and standard of proof

Once the defendant has raised the issue of consent, it is up to the prosecution to prove beyond reasonable doubt that the victim did not consent.

D Effect

A successful plea will result in the defendant's acquittal. Although consent cannot be used as a defence for murder, it can be used as a defence for manslaughter, sexual offences and non-fatal offences.

E Evaluation

1 *Irrational distinctions*

The cases of *Brown* and *Wilson* highlight the irrational distinctions that are often made between what appear to be similar situations. In *Brown*, the defence of consent was denied for charges of ABH and GBH caused by sexual activities. In Wilson, consent was allowed as a defence to ABH. Some critics have suggested that since the only real difference between the cases appears to be the sexual preferences of the parties involved, the decision was made on discriminatory grounds. Put simply, they claim that the defendants in *Brown* were denied the defence because they were homosexual. This view is assisted by the oft-cited quote from *Wilson*, when the Court of Appeal stated that: 'Consensual activity between husband and wife, in the privacy of the matrimonial home is not...a proper matter for criminal investigation.' While decisions continue to be made on a case-by-case basis, such distinctions are likely to continue.

2 *The law should not determine limits of personal autonomy*

Opponents of the current position question why it is up to the law to set limits on what individuals may or may not consent to. They claim that unelected judges, who are largely from a restricted social background, are not best placed to set limits on personal autonomy.

3 *Euthanasia*

Euthanasia is a contentious topic and has been the subject of many heated debates over the years. Currently, consent cannot operate as a defence to murder. Some argue that this is wrong, particularly when the suffering of terminally ill patients such as Diane Pretty is prolonged.

F Reform

The Law Commission reviewed the defence of consent in its 1995 paper 'Consent in the Criminal Law', but no significant reforms were suggested. It did remark that of the non-fatal offences only 'serious disabling injury' would not be allowed the defence of consent. If the Law Commission proposals became law, the defendants in *R* v *Brown and Others* (1993) would be allowed the defence of consent for charges of actual bodily harm.

Summary of Topic 6

Definition

Consent operates as a defence because the courts recognise that individuals have autonomy over their own lives. The general rule is that no liability is incurred if a person inflicts minor harm with the consent of the victim. However, there are limits as to what a person may consent to, and consent is not available as a defence to charges of murder or manslaughter.

Elements

Consent must be valid and informed. However, if the defendant has obtained the victim's consent by fraudulent means, this will not always render the consent invalid. Fraud will only invalidate consent if the victim is deceived as to the identity of the defendant or the nature and quality of his or her act. Consent can always be given to assault and battery, but when the charge is more serious, consent will only be valid if the activity provides a useful social purpose. The courts have developed a non-exhaustive list of acceptable activities people may consent to, including surgery, tattooing and piercing, properly conducted sports and horseplay, but not sadomasochistic homosexual activities.

Burden and standard of proof

Once the defendant has raised the issue of consent, it is up to the prosecution to prove beyond reasonable doubt that the victim did not consent.

Effect

A successful plea will result in the defendant's acquittal.

Evaluation

Irrational distinctions

Brown and *Wilson* highlight the irrational distinctions that are often made between what appear to be similar cases.

The law should not determine limits of personal autonomy

Some question why it is up to the law to set limits on what individuals may or may not consent to.

Euthanasia

Consent cannot operate as a defence to murder and some argue that this is wrong, particularly when the suffering of terminally ill patients is prolonged.

Reform

The Law Commission reviewed the defence of consent in its 1995 paper 'Consent in the Criminal Law', but no significant reforms were suggested.

TOPIC 7 Self-defence

This is a well-known type of defence. It has received much publicity over the years, particularly regarding the actions of householders who are confronted with intruders. The defence covers situations when force is needed to defend people or to prevent crime. However, tight restrictions are necessary to prevent people from taking the law into their own hands, and the force used must always be justified in the circumstances.

A Definition

There is a great deal of overlap between the three situations and similar principles apply to each.

There are three situations where the use of force may be justified: private defence, defence of property and prevention of crime.

1 *Private defence*

This is a common-law defence. It is often termed 'private defence', and includes defence of another person and defence of property.

2 *Defence of property*

This area is regulated partially by common law and partially by statute, namely the **Criminal Damage Act 1971** (see Topic 17).

3 *Prevention of crime*

This is a public or statutory defence. It is covered by the **Criminal Law Act 1967**, which states in s.3(1):

> A person may use such force as is reasonable in the circumstances in the prevention of crime, or in effecting or assisting in the lawful arrest of offenders or suspected offenders or of persons unlawfully at large.

B Elements

1 *Force must be necessary*

For force to be justified, it must have been necessary. The defendant is judged according to the circumstances as he or she honestly believed them to be. In order to decide whether force was necessary, the jury will consider the surrounding circumstances.

1.1 Pre-emptive strikes

Pre-emptive strikes are included within this defence. The defendant does not need to wait to be attacked before defending himself or herself.

***R* v *Beckford* (1988)**
In this case, Lord Griffith said: 'A man about to be attacked does not have to wait for his assailant to strike the first blow or fire the first shot; circumstances may justify a pre-emptive strike.'

A defendant can use threats of force or threats of death in order to try to stop an attack on himself or herself, or to prevent a crime.

***R* v *Cousins* (1982)**
The defendant believed that someone had taken out a contract on his life. He took a gun and went to see the father of the person whom he thought had arranged the contract. The defendant told the father that he would kill his son when he saw him. The defendant was convicted of making threats to kill, but on appeal the Court of Appeal said that such a threat might be lawful if it was reasonable in the circumstances.

1.2 Preparing for an attack

If the defendant believes that he or she is at risk from an attack on his or her person or property, he or she may be able to make preparations in order to defend himself or herself.

***Attorney General's Reference (No. 2)* (1983)**
The defendant's shop had been attacked during riots. To try to prevent this from happening again, he made petrol bombs that he intended to use should he face attack in the future. However, there was no further attack. The defendant was charged with breaching the **Explosive Substances Act 1883** by having an explosive substance in his possession. He relied on self-defence and was found not guilty under the Act. On appeal, his acquittal was upheld.

1.3 Duty to retreat

The courts had been called upon to consider whether a defendant is required to retreat from a situation if possible. In other words, self-defence would only be available to those who were unable to retreat. The question was whether, if faced with the choice, the defendant must retreat or if he or she could choose to stay and fight while still relying on self-defence. The issue was decided in the case of *R* v B*ird*.

***R* v *Bird* (1985)**
The defendant was at a party to celebrate her seventeenth birthday when her ex-boyfriend arrived with his new girlfriend. The defendant and her ex-boyfriend began to argue. He hit her and she retaliated, forgetting that she had a glass in her hand. The glass broke and caused serious injuries to the victim. The trial judge said that she could only rely on self-defence if she had shown an unwillingness to fight. The Court of Appeal disagreed with the trial judge. It decided that there

may be situations when the defendant might react immediately without retreating. The matter was for the jury to consider. This established that the defendant is not under a duty to retreat and may strike first in self-defence.

2 *Force must be reasonable*

Much of the debate surrounding this defence is concerned with whether the force used was reasonable in the circumstances. However, there is no definition of 'reasonable force' and it is a matter for the jury to decide in each case. The jury must take various factors into account, including the threat of harm, the urgency of the situation and any other options available to the defendant. A lower degree of force will be expected if the defendant is protecting property rather than people.

In *Palmer* (1971), it was held that a defendant did not have to 'weigh to a nicety the exact measure of his defensive action'. The jury must consider the fact that the defendant was acting in the heat of the moment, and as long as the defendant only did what he or she honestly thought was required, this will be evidence that the force used was reasonable. This is not a purely objective test, as the defendant's state of mind is to be considered. The reasonableness requirement means that it is not a purely subjective test either.

***R* v *Scarlett* (1993)**
The defendant was a pub landlord who tried to remove a drunken man from the pub. The man declined to leave voluntarily, and when the defendant believed that the drunk was about to hit him, he took him outside where the man fell backwards down some steps and died. The jury was directed that if it was satisfied that the defendant had used excessive force, he was guilty of manslaughter. The defendant appealed against his conviction on the grounds that he honestly believed the degree of force used was required. The Court of Appeal appeared to suggest that the test was subjective when it said that as long as the defendant thought that the circumstances called for the amount of force used, then he should not be convicted, 'even if his belief was unreasonable'.

This was tested in the case of *R* v *Owino*.

***R* v *Owino* (1995)**
The defendant punched his wife in the face repeatedly in order to restrain her. He was convicted of assault after the jury considered that he had used excessive force. On appeal, he tried to rely on *Scarlett* by arguing that he had a defence if he honestly believed that the amount of force used was reasonable, arguing that the test was subjective. The Court of Appeal upheld his conviction and said that the test was neither purely objective nor purely subjective. It stated that the test is whether a person used such force as was objectively reasonable in the circumstances as he or she believed them to be.

This test was confirmed in *R* v *Martin*.

***R* v *Martin* (2002)**
This case received much media attention. The defendant was a farmer who lived on an isolated farm. One night, two burglars broke into the farmhouse and the

Remember, there is no definition of 'reasonable force'. It is up to the jury to decide in each case.

defendant shot them, killing one and wounding the other. At his trial, he sought to rely on self-defence. However, this was rejected by the jury, as it was felt that he had used excessive force, for example by not firing a warning shot. The defence asked the Court of Appeal to take into account the defendant's paranoid personality disorder that led him to believe that he was in greater danger than he actually was. The Court of Appeal held that while physical characteristics of the defendant could be taken into account, psychiatric characteristics could only be considered in exceptional circumstances. This case did not fall into the definition of exceptional circumstances, but Martin's murder conviction was quashed on the basis of diminished responsibility.

3 Use of excessive force

Martin was unable to rely on self-defence as he had used excessive force to defend himself. Self-defence is an 'all or nothing' defence, which means that if it is pleaded successfully, the defendant is acquitted, but if the jury believes that the force was excessive in the circumstances, then it fails and the defendant is found guilty. This has been criticised, as the defendant who rightly thinks that force is needed but makes a mistake as to the degree necessary will not be able to rely on the defence.

***R* v *Clegg* (1995)**
The defendant was a soldier in Belfast. A stolen car drove through a checkpoint without stopping and he fired at it, killing one of the passengers. His murder conviction was upheld, as the car had passed through the checkpoint when the fatal shot was fired. As the danger had passed by this point, force was no longer required.

4 Mistake as to the need for self-defence

If a defendant makes a mistake and thinks that self-defence is necessary, he or she will be judged on the facts as he or she honestly believed them to be. This is still the case if the mistake was unreasonable.

***R* v *Williams (Gladstone)* (1984)**
A man, Mason, saw another man trying to rob a woman in the street. He chased after the man and managed to grab him. At this point, the defendant came upon the scene. He had not seen the earlier robbery and mistakenly thought that Mason was the attacker. Mason lied and told the defendant that he was in the police. The defendant asked to see his warrant card and when Mason was unable to produce it, the defendant punched him. During his trial for ABH, the defendant said that he had mistakenly thought that Mason was attacking the other man. He had therefore stepped in to defend the 'victim'. The judge directed the jury that a mistake had to be both honest and reasonable. On appeal, the defendant's conviction was quashed. The court held that his mistake had to be honest but need not be reasonable. Obviously, though, the more unreasonable the belief, the less likely the jury is to believe that the defendant honestly held it.

5 *Intoxication and self-defence*

If the defendant was intoxicated when making the mistake as to the need for self-defence, the rule on mistake changes.

***R* v *O'Grady* (1987)**
The defendant had been drinking with his friend. At his trial, he said that he had woken up in the night to find his friend hitting him. He retaliated and then went back to sleep. He awoke later the following morning to find his friend dead. His plea of self-defence failed. On appeal, his conviction for manslaughter was upheld. The Court of Appeal said that a mistake due to voluntary intoxication could not form the basis of a defence to any crime.

C Burden and standard of proof

Once the defendant has raised the issue of self-defence or there is some other evidence of it, it is up to the prosecution to prove beyond reasonable doubt that the defendant was not acting in self-defence or that the force used was unreasonable.

D Effect

If a defendant acts to protect himself or herself, another individual or property, then providing that the force used is reasonable, he or she has a complete defence to any crime, since the justifiable use of force means his or her actions are not unlawful. Thus, if successful, he or she will be found not guilty.

E Evaluation

1 *The 'all or nothing' effect*

As mentioned above, a situation may arise where some force is justified but the defendant uses too much. This means that the defence fails, and critics have argued that this can lead to unfair results. For some offences, the need for some force can be taken into account when sentencing the defendant. In murder cases, however, the mandatory nature of the sentence means that this is not possible and the defendant will be convicted and sentenced to life imprisonment. This was seen in the cases of *Clegg* and *Martin* (see above).

2 *Intoxication*

The current rule is that a defendant will not be able to rely on a mistaken belief that self-defence is required if that mistake was made due to intoxication (see

O'Grady). This has been criticised as being too harsh, particularly given that intoxication is a defence to specific intent crimes (see Topic 10).

F Reform

1 Allow an alternative conviction of manslaughter

To combat criticism of the 'all or nothing' nature of the defence, it has been suggested that, where some force is justified but the defendant uses too much and causes the death of the victim, it should be open to the jury to convict the defendant of manslaughter rather than murder. This argument was rejected in *Clegg*, but the Law Commission, in its consultation document 'Partial Defences To Murder' (2003), suggested that this area needed to be re-examined.

2 Change the ruling in O'Grady

The rule in *O'Grady* is seen by some as too harsh, and it has been suggested that mistakes as to the need for self-defence induced by intoxication *should* operate as a defence.

Summary of Topic 7

Definition

There are three situations where the use of force may be justified: private defence, defence of property and prevention of crime.

Private defence

This is a common-law defence. It is often termed 'private defence', and includes defence of another person and defence of property.

Defence of property

This area is regulated partially by common law and partially by statute, namely the **Criminal Damage Act 1971**.

Prevention of crime

This is a public or statutory defence covered by the **Criminal Law Act 1967**, which states in s.3(1):

> A person may use such force as is reasonable in the circumstances in the prevention of crime, or in effecting or assisting in the lawful arrest of offenders or suspected offenders or of persons unlawfully at large.

There is a great deal of overlap between the three situations and similar principles apply to each.

Elements

For force to be justified, it must have been necessary. The defendant is judged according to the circumstances as he or she honestly believed them to be. To decide whether force was necessary, the jury will consider the surrounding circumstances. The force must also be reasonable — this is a matter for the jury in each case.

Premptive strikes

Pre-emptive strikes are permissible, so a person does not have to wait to be attacked before defending himself or herself. A defendant can use threats of force or threats of death in order to try to stop an attack on himself or herself, or to prevent a crime.

Preparing for an attack

If the defendant believes that he or she is at risk of an attack on his or her person or property, he or she may be able to make preparations in order to defend himself or herself.

Duty to retreat

A defendant is not under a duty to retreat. If a defendant makes a mistake and thinks that self-defence is necessary, he or she will be judged on the facts as he or she honestly believed them to be. This is still the case if the mistake was unreasonable. However, if the defendant uses excessive force, the defence will fail.

Burden and standard of proof

Once the defendant has raised the issue of self-defence or there is some other evidence of it, it is up to the prosecution to prove beyond reasonable doubt that the defendant was not acting in self-defence or that the force used was unreasonable.

Effect

If a defendant acts to protect himself or herself, another individual or property, then providing that the force used is reasonable, he or she has a complete defence to any crime, since the justifiable use of force means his or her actions are not unlawful.

Evaluation

The 'all or nothing' effect

Some force may be justified in a given situation, but if the defendant uses too much, the defence fails. Critics have argued that this can lead to unfair results. In murder cases, the mandatory nature of the sentence means that the defendant will be convicted and face life imprisonment.

Intoxication

The current rule is that a defendant will not be able to rely on a mistaken belief that self-defence is required if that mistake was made due to intoxication. This has been considered too harsh, particularly given that intoxication is a defence to specific intent crimes.

Reform

Allow an alternative conviction of manslaughter

To combat criticism of the 'all or nothing' nature of the defence, it has been suggested that, where some force is justified but the defendant uses too much and causes the death of the victim, it should be open to the jury to convict him or her of manslaughter rather than murder.

Change the ruling in *O'Grady*

The rule in *O'Grady* is seen by some as too harsh, and it has been suggested that mistakes as to the need for self-defence induced by intoxication *should* operate as a defence.

TOPIC 8 Insanity

The defence of insanity is concerned with the mental capacity of the defendant. It has long been the case that in order to be criminally liable, a defendant must be deemed sane.

A Definition

The current rules regarding insanity come from the case of *M'Naghten* (1843). The starting point is that everyone is presumed sane, as it would be too onerous a burden if the prosecution had to prove a defendant's sanity or otherwise in every case.

***R* v *M'Naghten* (1843)**
The defendant suffered from paranoia and thought that the government was persecuting him. He decided to kill the prime minister, Robert Peel, but killed Peel's secretary instead. Medical experts gave evidence to the effect that he was insane. There was a public outcry when the jury accepted this evidence and acquitted the defendant.

This case lead to the courts attempting to clarify the defence of insanity and their explanation became known as the 'M'Naghten rules', which have formed the basis of the defence ever since.

In order to establish a defence on the grounds of insanity, it must be clearly proved that at the time of committing the act the defendant was labouring under such a defect of reason, caused by a disease of the mind, that he or she either did not know the nature and quality of the act or did not know that what he or she was doing was legally wrong.

B Elements

1 *Defect of reason*

The defendant must show that he or she was suffering from a defect of reason; in other words, that his or her ability to reason was impaired. This is because the basis of the defence is the defendant's deprivation of the power of reasoning. Thus, a defendant who still possessed those powers but failed to use them cannot be classed as insane.

***R* v *Clarke* (1972)**
The defendant was charged with theft after taking items from a supermarket without paying for them. She claimed that she was suffering from depression that had caused her to be absent-minded and she did not remember putting the items in her bag. She was denying the *mens rea* element of the defence, but the trial

judge ruled that this amounted to a plea of insanity. In order to avoid indefinite detention in a hospital, she then pleaded guilty. On appeal her conviction was overturned. The court accepted that she still possessed powers of reasoning, it was just that she had failed to use them in this instance.

2 Disease of the mind

In this context, 'disease of the mind' is a legal and not a medical term. This has caused problems at times, since the legal definition does not always match the medical definition. This is apparent when looking at the types of conditions that the courts have accepted as constituting a disease of the mind. Obviously, following *M'Naghten*, delusional states are covered by this, but the inclusion of certain other conditions has caused controversy.

Remember that the term 'disease of the mind' is very broad and can include both mental and physical conditions.

***R* v *Kemp* (1957)**
The arteriosclerosis (hardening of the arteries) suffered by the defendant caused loss of control, during which he attacked his wife with a hammer. This is clearly a physical rather than a mental condition, but the courts held that it still constituted a disease of the mind. This was because the condition had affected the defendant's 'mind', which in this case was taken to mean his memory as well as his ability to reason and understand, rather than simply his physical brain.

***R* v *Sullivan* (1984)**
The defendant was epileptic and attacked a neighbour during a fit. At his trial, he sought to rely on the defence of non-insane automatism, but it was held that his epilepsy constituted a 'disease of the mind'. He changed his plea to guilty to avoid indefinite hospitalisation. On appeal, both the Court of Appeal and the House of Lords upheld his conviction and maintained that epilepsy did constitute a disease of the mind for the purposes of insanity, as the defendant's mental abilities were impaired.

***R* v *Hennessy* (1989)**
The defendant was a diabetic but had not taken his insulin for a number of days. He had been disqualified from driving but was seen driving a stolen car. At his trial, he claimed that he had been suffering from hyperglycaemia at the time of the offence and did not remember the incident. The judge ruled that this constituted a plea of insanity and the defendant changed his plea to guilty. On appeal, his conviction was upheld.

***R* v *Burgess* (1991)**
The defendant attacked his girlfriend while sleepwalking. He tried to rely on the defence of automatism but the judge at his trial held that the correct defence was that of insanity. His conviction was upheld on appeal.

***Bratty* v *Attorney General for Northern Ireland* (1963)**
The defendant strangled his victim during an epileptic seizure. This was treated as a plea of insanity by the courts. The House of Lords held that any mental disorder that is prone to recur should be classed as a 'disease of the mind'.

3 Did not know the nature and quality of the act or that the act was wrong

The cases detailed above show the broad meaning that the courts attribute to the term 'disease of the mind'. What the conditions have in common is that they are all considered by the courts to be caused by an internal factor. The idea is that, since such conditions are internal, they are likely to reoccur, making the defendant a continuing danger to the public. The courts have therefore preferred to label defendants as insane, which means they can be detained in hospital, rather than allowing an acquittal under the defence of automatism (see Topic 9).

The defect of reason caused by a disease of the mind must mean either that the defendant does not know the nature and quality of his or her act, or, if he or she does, that he or she does not know that the act is legally wrong.

In terms of the 'nature and quality of the act', the defendant would be unaware of his or her actions. An example that is often given is of a defendant who thinks that he or she is cutting a loaf of bread but who is in actual fact cutting the victim's throat. If the defendant is aware of what he or she is doing, he or she may still rely on the defence of insanity if he or she does not know that the act is legally wrong.

***R* v *Windle* (1952)**
The defendant gave his wife a fatal overdose of aspirin. He said to the police: 'I suppose they will hang me for this.' This proved that he knew what he was doing was legally wrong so he was unable to rely on the defence of insanity. His murder conviction was upheld by the Court of Appeal.

C Burden and standard of proof

The defendant must prove that he or she was suffering from insanity when he or she committed the offence. This must be proved on the balance of probabilities.

D Effect

If a plea is successful, it leads to a special verdict and the defendant will be deemed 'not guilty by reason of insanity'. Until the introduction of the **Criminal Procedure Act 1991**, this automatically meant an indefinite hospital stay, but now this only applies to murder. If the defendant is charged with another crime, the judge can make a hospital order, a guardianship order, a supervision and treatment order or an absolute discharge.

E Evaluation

1 The burden of proof rests with the defendant

Critics have argued that it is unfair that the burden is on the defendant to prove, on the balance of probabilities, that he or she was suffering from insanity. They say that this undermines the notion that the defendant is innocent until proven guilty by the prosecution.

2 The use of a legal rather than a medical definition

Perhaps the major flaw in this defence is that the courts use a legal definition of insanity rather than a medical one. In addition, this definition dates from 1843, and remains firmly rooted in that era in terms of its understanding of insanity, failing to take account of the huge changes that have occurred since those times.

3 The rules are too broad

The classification of diabetics, epileptics and sleepwalkers as insane has been criticised for suggesting that those suffering from such conditions are a danger to the public, whereas this is far from the truth in the vast majority of cases. Most people with such conditions are able to control them successfully by taking medication.

4 The rules are too narrow

The defence can rule out those who are medically insane if they know the nature and quality of their act or that it is legally wrong, but are nonetheless unable to stop themselves from committing it. Thus, those at whom the defence should be aimed are unable to rely on it.

F Reform

1 Place the burden of proof on the prosecution

Both the Butler Committee and the Criminal Law Revision Committee have suggested that, since it is part of *mens rea*, the burden of proof should be reversed and placed on the prosecution rather than on the defendant.

2 A new defence

Critics argue that the only way forward is to abolish the M'Naghten rules altogether. Instead, a new defence should be introduced. The Butler Committee suggested that this should apply to defendants with a mental disorder and should result in a verdict of 'not guilty on evidence of a mental disorder'. This would avoid the defendant being labelled insane. Others suggest that there is no need for such a defence at all and that those suffering from insanity should be dealt with outside the criminal justice system.

Summary of Topic 8

Definition

In order to establish a defence on the grounds of insanity, it must be clearly proved that at the time of committing the act the party accused was labouring under such a defect of reason, caused by a disease of the mind, that he or she either did not know the nature and quality of the act or did not know that what he or she was doing was legally wrong.

Elements

The defendant must show that he or she was suffering from a defect of reason; in other words, that his or her ability to reason was impaired. A defendant who still possessed those powers but failed to use them cannot be classed as insane.

The defect of reason must be caused by 'disease of the mind'. This is a legal rather than a medical term, and the two do not always coincide. The legal nature of the term is apparent when looking at the types of conditions that the courts have accepted as constituting a disease of the mind, including hardening of the arteries, epilepsy, diabetes and sleepwalking.

The defect of reason must mean either that the defendant does not know the nature and quality of the act (i.e. is unaware of his or her actions), or, if he or she does, he or she does not know that the act is legally wrong.

Burden and standard of proof

The defendant must prove that he or she was suffering from insanity when he or she committed the offence. This must be proved on the balance of probabilities.

Effect

If a plea is successful, it leads to a special verdict and the defendant will be deemed 'not guilty by reason of insanity'. Until the introduction of the **Criminal Procedure Act 1991**, this verdict automatically meant an indefinite hospital stay, but now this only applies to murder. If the defendant is charged with another crime, the judge can make a hospital order, a guardianship order, a supervision and treatment order or an absolute discharge.

Evaluation

The burden of proof rests with the defendant

Critics have argued it is unfair that the burden of proof is on the defendant, as this undermines the notion that the defendant is innocent until proven guilty.

The use of a legal rather than a medical definition

The major flaw in the defence is that the courts use a legal definition of insanity rather than a medical one. In addition, the legal definition comes from 1843 and fails to take into account the huge medical advances that have occurred since then.

The rules are too broad

The classification of diabetics, epileptics and sleepwalkers as insane has been criticised, since it suggests that those suffering from such conditions are a danger to the public, whereas this is far from the truth in the vast majority of cases.

The rules are too narrow

The defence can rule out those who are medically insane if they know the nature and quality of their act or that it is legally wrong, but are nonetheless unable to stop themselves from committing it.

Reform

Place the burden of proof on the prosecution

Both the Butler Committee and the Criminal Law Revision Committee have suggested that, since it is part of *mens rea*, the burden of proof should be reversed and placed on the prosecution rather than on the defendant.

A new defence

Critics argue that the only way forward is to abolish the M'Naghten rules altogether. Instead, a new defence should be introduced. The Butler Committee suggested that this should apply to defendants with a mental disorder and should result in a verdict of 'not guilty on evidence of a mental disorder'. Others suggest that there is no need for such a defence at all and that those suffering from insanity should be dealt with outside the criminal justice system.

TOPIC 9 Automatism

It is important to understand the distinction between insanity and automatism and the different effect each will have on a defendant, as this is a popular area for examination questions.

While insanity is often referred to as 'insane automatism', this defence is sometimes known as 'sane automatism'. The two defences are closely linked; indeed, many defendants seeking to rely on automatism have found themselves being classed as insane.

A Definition

The basis of this defence is the defendant's inability to control his or her actions.

***Bratty* v *Attorney General for Northern Ireland* (1963)**
In this case, Lord Denning defined automatism as 'an act which is done by the muscles without any control by the mind'. Examples given included a spasm, reflex action, and an act induced by concussion.

It has long been accepted that a defendant will only face criminal liability for his or her actions if they were performed voluntarily. With the defence of automatism, a defendant claims that the *actus reus* was involuntary and argues that therefore he or she should not be convicted of the offence. Since the defendant is denying the *actus reus*, automatism may be used as a defence to all crimes, including those classed as strict liability offences.

B Elements

1 *Total loss of voluntary control*

The defendant must show that there was a complete loss of voluntary control in order to rely on automatism.

***Broome* v *Perkins* (1987)**
The defendant was in a hypoglycaemic state due to diabetes. He was convicted of driving without due care and attention after driving erratically and crashing into another car. At his trial, he sought to rely on automatism as a defence. The defence failed, however, as the court held that he had not suffered a total loss of control. There was evidence that he had shown sufficient control over his actions in order to brake and steer his car.

***Attorney General's Reference (No. 2)* (1992)**
The defendant was a lorry driver who drifted onto the hard shoulder of a motorway and killed two people. At his trial, he produced medical evidence of a condition known as 'driving without awareness', which was induced by long journeys on straight roads. On appeal by the prosecution, the Court of Appeal held that automatism should not have been available, as the defendant had demonstrated at least partial control over the lorry.

2 Loss of control must be caused by an external factor

The total loss of control must be due to an external factor. This is the key difference between insanity and automatism. Thus, for a successful plea of automatism, the defendant must show that his or her involuntary act was caused by an external factor.

The courts have given examples of what constitutes an external factor, including:

- a blow to the head causing concussion
- being stung by a bee (a famous example given in *Hill* v *Baxter*)
- being given anaesthetic
- a reflex action
- being hypnotised
- suffering from severe shock or post-traumatic stress disorder

A point to note is that Quick's doctor stated during the trial that Quick had been admitted to hospital a number of times due to hypoglycaemia. If the case were to be heard today, his condition might be regarded as being self-induced. This could stop him from relying on the defence (see part 3 below).

***R* v *Quick* (1973)**
The defendant was a nurse. He suffered from diabetes, and while in a hypoglycaemic state, he attacked one of his patients. At trial, he said that he had taken his insulin but had not eaten and had also been drinking — all external factors. He had no recollection of the attack. The trial judge ruled that the correct defence was that of insanity and Quick then pleaded guilty. On appeal, his conviction was quashed and it was held that automatism should have been left to the jury — his condition had been induced by external rather than internal factors.

***R* v *T* (1990)**
The defendant was charged with robbery and ABH. At her trial, it transpired that she had been raped just a few days earlier and medical evidence was introduced to show that she was suffering from post-traumatic stress disorder as a result. She was said to be in a 'dissociative state' at the time of the offences and as such had not been acting consciously. The judge ruled that she was able to rely on the defence of automatism, since her state of mind was caused by the external event of the rape.

3 Self-induced automatism

If the automatism was caused by voluntary consumption of drugs or alcohol, the defendant cannot rely on this defence and will be subject to the rules of intoxication instead. This is clearly a policy decision.

***R* v *Lipman* (1970)**
The defendant and his girlfriend had taken LSD. They fell asleep, but during the night the defendant began to hallucinate and believed he was being attacked by snakes. In the morning, he awoke to find that his girlfriend had been strangled and their bed sheets had been pushed down her throat. Although the defendant was clearly in a state of automatism when he killed his girlfriend, he was unable to rely on the defence as the courts held that it was not available if the defendant's state was self-induced by drink or drugs.

If the defendant's automatism is caused by something other than drink or drugs, he or she *may* be able to use the defence, although this is dependent on whether he or she knew there was a risk of getting into such a condition.

***R* v *Bailey* (1983)**

This is a similar case to *Quick* but the outcome was different. The defendant was a diabetic who had taken his insulin. He visited his ex-girlfriend and her new boyfriend. While he was there, he felt unwell. He drank a mixture of sugar and water, but did not eat anything. About 10 minutes afterwards, he hit the new boyfriend on the head with an iron bar. At trial, he claimed to have been unable to control his actions because of his hypoglycaemic state. The judge ruled that automatism was not available as the defendant's condition had been self-induced through not eating. On appeal, it was held that he could use automatism as a defence to the s.18 **Offences Against the Persons Act 1861** (OAPA) charge as it was a specific intent crime. His automatic state was evidence that the defendant did not have *mens rea*. On the alternative s.20 OAPA charge, the court held that automatism did not provide a defence, as the defendant had been reckless by failing to eat after taking his insulin.

The position following this case is that self-induced automatism (other than that caused by drink or drugs) is a defence to crimes of specific intent. It may operate as a defence to crimes of basic intent if the prosecution cannot prove that the defendant was recklessness. Whether the defendant is reckless or not will depend on whether he or she knew that his or her acts or omissions were likely to make him or her aggressive or unpredictable. If the defendant in *Bailey* was aware that not eating after taking his insulin would make him aggressive, then he could be said to be reckless in failing to eat.

C Burden and standard of proof

If the defendant seeks to rely on automatism, he or she must raise the defence and will usually require medical evidence in order to do so. Once the defence has been raised, it is for the prosecution to disprove.

D Effect

Automatism acts as a complete defence and a successful plea means that the defendant will be found not guilty.

E Evaluation

1 *Leads to irrational and unfair results*

The courts have tried to restrict the availability of automatism because it results in a complete acquittal, despite the fact that the defendant may have beaten someone up (*Quick*) or committed ABH and robbery (*R* v *T*). By making it as hard

Use examples from the cases cited in this topic and in Topic 8, including *Broome* v *Perkins*, *Sullivan* and *Burgess*, to highlight the injustice that can be caused. You should also contrast *Quick* and *Hennessy* to show how two defendants suffering from the same condition were treated in very different ways.

as possible to rely on as a defence, they hope that only genuine automatons can use it. This is understandable, but can have harsh results.

The distinctions made between internal and external factors have been criticised in cases such as *Quick* and *Hennessey*. In these cases, both defendants suffered from diabetes, but in *Quick*, the attack was blamed on the defendant taking insulin and not eating — classed as an external factor — so he could rely on automatism. In *Hennessey*, the defendant's condition was due to his failure to take his insulin. His condition was classed as being caused by his diabetes, which was an internal factor, and he was therefore considered insane.

The main justification behind the distinction is that an internal factor is more likely to reoccur than an external one, and thus the public is more likely to be at risk from a defendant with such a condition. Critics argue that this may be true if someone is suffering from mental illness and attacks someone; he or she may be more likely to do it again than someone who attacks the victim after a knock to the head. However, in the diabetic cases, both defendants were suffering from the same disease so the distinction is illogical.

F Reform

1 *Extending automatism*

It has been suggested that the defence of automatism should be extended to cover all cases that can be controlled by drugs or eating and drinking, e.g. epilepsy and diabetes. This would go some way to reducing the illogical distinctions that are often made. The Law Commission's Criminal Code Bill also proposes the inclusion of sleepwalking under the defence. This would change the ruling in *Burgess*, where the condition was classed as insanity, and follows the Canadian case of *Parks*. In this case, a defendant who drove several miles to the home of his in-laws and murdered his mother-in-law while sleepwalking successfully relied on automatism and was acquitted.

2 *Abolishing internal and external factors*

Some have suggested going a stage further and abolishing the notion of internal and external factors. Before this could be done, however, the law on insanity would need to be updated.

Summary of Topic 9

Definition

With the defence of automatism, a defendant claims that the *actus reus* was involuntary and argues that therefore he or she should not be convicted of the offence. Since the defendant is denying the *actus reus*, automatism may be used as a defence to all crimes, including those classed as strict liability offences.

Elements

The defendant must show that there was a complete loss of voluntary control due to an external factor. This is the key difference between insanity and automatism. The courts have given examples of what constitutes an external factor; these include a blow to the head, being stung by a bee, being given anaesthetic, a reflex action, being hypnotised and suffering from severe shock or post-traumatic stress disorder.

If the automatism was caused by voluntary consumption of drugs or alcohol, the defendant cannot rely on the defence and will be subject to the rules of intoxication instead. If the defendant's automatism is caused by something other than drink or drugs, he or she *may* be able to use the defence, although this is dependent upon whether he or she knew there was a risk of getting into such a condition.

Burden and standard of proof

The defendant must raise the defence and will usually require medical evidence in order to do so. Once the defence has been raised, it is for the prosecution to disprove.

Effect

Automatism acts as a complete defence and a successful plea means that the defendant will be found not guilty.

Evaluation

Leads to irrational and unfair results

The courts have tried to restrict the availability of automatism because it results in a complete acquittal, despite the fact that the defendant has committed what would otherwise be a crime.

The courts have ensured that it is difficult to rely on the defence, but this can have harsh results. The distinction made between internal and external factors has been criticised in cases such as *Quick* and *Hennessey*. In these cases both defendants suffered from diabetes, but only one of them could rely on automatism. The main justification behind the distinction is that an internal factor is more likely to reoccur than an external one, and thus the public is more likely to be at risk from a defendant with such a condition. Critics argue that this may be true if someone is suffering from mental illness and attacks someone — he or she may be more likely to do it again than someone who attacks a victim after a knock to the head — but, in the diabetic cases, both were suffering from the same disease so the distinction is illogical.

Reform

Extending automatism

It has been suggested that the defence of automatism should be extended to cover all cases that can be controlled by drugs or eating and drinking, e.g. epilepsy and diabetes. This would go some way to reducing the illogical distinctions that are often made.

The Law Commission's Criminal Code Bill also proposes the inclusion of sleepwalking under the defence.

Abolishing internal and external factors

Some have suggested going a stage further and abolishing the notion of internal and external factors. Before this could be done, however, the law on insanity would need to be updated.

TOPIC 10 Intoxication

The defence of intoxication is a matter of great debate. Legal principle requires that defendants incapable of forming *mens rea* be acquitted, while public policy demands that they are not.

A Definition

A defendant can become intoxicated by means of alcohol or drugs or both together. The essence of the defence is that the defendant was so intoxicated that he or she was incapable of forming the *mens rea* of the offence that he or she is charged with. The defendant who gets drunk or takes drugs and then does something that he or she would not otherwise have done will not be able to rely on the defence. Since the effect of the intoxication must be to render the defendant incapable of anticipating any of the consequences of his or her actions, the defence will only apply in limited circumstances, where the effect of the intoxication was extreme.

Remember that the defendant is denying having *mens rea*.

B Elements

1 *Absence of* mens rea

The defendant must show that the alcohol, drugs or combination of the two made him or her incapable of forming the *mens rea* of the relevant offence. If, despite his or her intoxicated state, the defendant was still able to form the necessary *mens rea*, the defence will not apply (see *Kingston* below).

2 *Voluntary and involuntary intoxication*

The courts draw a distinction between voluntary and involuntary intoxication.

2.1 Voluntary intoxication

This applies to the defendant who has voluntarily consumed alcohol or drugs commonly known to make people aggressive or out of control. If he or she is incapable of forming the necessary *mens rea*, the defendant will have a defence to specific but not basic intent crimes.

2.2 Involuntary intoxication

Make sure that you recognise the difference between voluntary and involuntary intoxication.

A defendant may be classed as being involuntarily intoxicated. This can arise in a number of situations:

- The defendant was 'spiked' without his or her knowledge, and was therefore unaware that he or she was consuming drugs or alcohol.
- The defendant took prescription drugs.
- The defendant had an unexpected reaction to soporific drugs.

***R* v *Hardie* (1984)**

After arguing with his girlfriend, the defendant took some of her Valium tablets to calm his nerves. Valium is a sedative and its usual effect is to make the person sleepy. In this case, however, it failed to have the usual effect, and while under its influence, the defendant set fire to his flat. On appeal, his conviction under the **Criminal Damage Act 1971** was overturned. The Court of Appeal said that since the usual effect of the drug was soporific, the defendant was not reckless in taking it if he was unaware that it would have an unexpected effect upon him.

Thus, if the defendant is involuntarily intoxicated, he or she will have a defence to both specific and basic intent crimes, as long as he or she did not form the required *mens rea*.

If, despite an intoxicated state, he or she was still able to form *mens rea*, he or she will have no defence, even if the intoxication is involuntary. In *R* v *Sheehan and Moore* (1975), it was stressed that 'a drunken intent is nevertheless an intent'.

***R* v *Kingston* (1994)**

The defendant was a known paedophile. A business associate set out to blackmail him and invited him round to his flat. Once there, his drink was spiked and he was taken to a room where a 15-year-old boy was asleep and told to abuse him. The defendant did so and his associate photographed the attack. The House of Lords upheld his conviction for indecent assault, despite the fact that his intoxication was involuntary. This was because the defendant admitted that he had intended to assault the boy. He was therefore guilty since he had formed the relevant *mens rea*, despite his intoxicated state.

***R* v *Allen* (1988)**

The defendant voluntarily drank wine but it was much stronger than he had realised. The court held that his lack of knowledge of its alcoholic strength was not enough to render his intoxication involuntary — he had drunk it voluntarily, knowing that it was wine.

3 Specific and basic intent crimes

Even if the defendant proves that he or she lacked *mens rea*, he or she can still be found liable for some crimes. The courts have also drawn a distinction between crimes of specific intent and crimes of basic intent.

3.1 Specific intent crimes

Generally, a crime of specific intent is one where the *mens rea* is intention only. Examples of specific intent crimes are:

- murder
- s.18 **Offences Against the Person Act 1861**
- theft
- robbery
- burglary

Voluntary and involuntary intoxication both provide a defence to specific intent crimes.

3.2 Basic intent crimes

With basic intent crimes, the *mens rea* can include recklessness. Examples of basic intent crimes include:

- involuntary manslaughter
- s.20 Offences Against the Person Act
- s.47 Offences Against the Person Act
- assault
- battery

If the defendant is voluntarily intoxicated, he or she will not have a defence to a crime of specific intent if he or she has been reckless. Involuntary intoxication, on the other hand, will provide a defence to basic intent crimes.

Make sure that you understand the difference between specific and basic intent crimes and can give examples of each.

For most offences of specific intent, there is a similar basic intent crime. For example, if the defendant is charged with murder and pleads intoxication, he or she may be charged with the basic intent crime of manslaughter instead. If the defendant is not guilty of s.18 OAPA due to voluntary intoxication, he or she may be guilty of s.20 OAPA instead. However, not all specific intent offences have a corresponding basic intent crime, and in these cases intoxication can be a complete defence. An example of such an offence is theft.

***DPP* v *Majewski* (1977)**
The defendant had been drinking and taking drugs for a number of hours when he became involved in a fight. He was charged with a number of counts of assault against members of the public and the police officers who had been trying to arrest him. At his trial, he claimed that he could not remember anything of the incident due to the effects of the alcohol and drugs that he had taken. The House of Lords held that voluntary intoxication could not provide a defence to crimes of basic intent and he was therefore guilty.

4 *'Dutch courage'*

If someone deliberately gets intoxicated to give himself or herself 'Dutch courage' to commit a crime, his or her intoxication will not be a defence to any crime — even to crimes that can only be committed with a specific intention.

***Attorney General for Northern Ireland* v *Gallagher* (1963)**
The defendant wanted to kill his wife. He bought a knife and a bottle of whisky, which he drank in order to give himself 'Dutch courage'. Once sufficiently intoxicated, he stabbed and killed his wife with the knife. The House of Lords upheld his conviction for murder since, on the evidence, he had formed the *mens rea* at the relevant time.

C Burden and standard of proof

The burden of proof rests with the defendant. He or she must provide some evidence of intoxication before the defence can be put before the jury. It is then up to the prosecution to prove beyond reasonable doubt that, despite this evidence, the defendant still formed the necessary *mens rea*.

D Effect

The effect of intoxication varies according to the type of crime that the defendant is charged with and whether the defendant was voluntarily or involuntarily intoxicated.

If the defendant was voluntarily intoxicated and incapable of forming *mens rea*, he or she has a defence to specific intent crimes but not crimes of basic intent. If the defendant is charged with a specific intent crime that does not have a corresponding basic intent crime, e.g. theft, intoxication can provide a complete defence.

If the defendant is involuntarily intoxicated and incapable of forming *mens rea*, he or she will have a defence to both basic and specific intent crimes.

E Evaluation

1 *Distinction between basic and specific intent crimes*

It is difficult to know for certain which offences the courts will class as specific intent crimes and which they will class as basic intent crimes. This is because the general rule of basic/specific intent crimes classification is not always consistently applied. Critics argue that the distinction should be abandoned and the matter left in the hands of the jury in each case. Others argue that since the defendant pleading intoxication was unable to form *mens rea*, he or she should not be held criminally liable at all. However, policy issues would probably prevent this from ever happening.

2 *Inconsistency in its effect*

Some specific intent crimes, such as theft, do not have a corresponding basic intent crime. Intoxication therefore operates as a complete defence to those crimes. However, for specific intent crimes that *do* have a corresponding basic intent offence, the defendant will be convicted. For example, if the defendant is charged with theft but successfully pleads intoxication he or she will be acquitted, as there is no corresponding basic intent crime with which he or she can be charged. If a defendant is charged with murder, however, and successfully pleads intoxication, he or she will be convicted of manslaughter instead. Furthermore, there is no logical reason why some crimes have a corresponding offence while others do not.

F Reform

1 *Ensuring that all specific intent crimes have a corresponding basic intent offence*

It has been suggested that the current distinction between basic and specific offences should be maintained, as long as all crimes of specific intent are given a corresponding basic intent crime.

2 *Intoxication offence*

The Butler Committee suggested that the current law should be replaced with a new offence of 'dangerous intoxication'. Juries could then find a defendant guilty of 'dangerous intoxication' rather than the offence committed. A maximum penalty of 1 year was suggested for a first offence, rising to 3 years for any further convictions.

3 *Full defence*

Critics have argued that since the defendant was incapable of forming *mens rea*, legal principle dictates that he or she should be acquitted. This means that intoxication would operate as a complete defence to any crime. This is the position in Australia, but policy considerations mean that the approach is unlikely to be followed in the UK.

Summary of Topic 10

Definition

A defendant can become intoxicated by means of alcohol or drugs or both together. The essence of the defence is that the defendant was so intoxicated that he or she was incapable of forming the *mens rea* of the offence that he or she is charged with. The defendant who gets drunk or takes drugs and then does something that he or she would not otherwise have done will not be able to rely on the defence. The defence will only apply in limited circumstances, where the effect of the intoxication was extreme.

Elements

Absence of *mens rea*

The defendant must show that the alcohol, drugs or combination of the two made him or her incapable of forming the *mens rea* of the relevant offence. If, despite his or her intoxicated state, the defendant was still able to form the necessary *mens rea*, the defence will not apply.

Voluntary and involuntary intoxication

The courts draw a distinction between voluntary and involuntary intoxication.

- Voluntary intoxication applies to the defendant who has voluntarily consumed alcohol or drugs commonly known to make people aggressive or out of control.

- A defendant may be classed as being involuntarily intoxicated if he or she was 'spiked' and therefore unaware that he or she was consuming drugs or alcohol, if he or she took prescription drugs or had an unexpected reaction to soporific drugs.

Even if the defendant proves that he or she lacked *mens rea*, he or she can still be found liable for some crimes.

Specific and basic intent crimes

The courts have drawn a distinction between crimes of specific intent and crimes of basic intent.

Specific intent crimes

Generally, a crime of specific intent is one where the *mens rea* is intention only. Examples of specific intent crimes are murder, s.18 OAPA 1861, theft, robbery and burglary. Voluntary and involuntary intoxication both provide a defence to specific intent crimes.

Basic intent crimes

With basic intent crimes, the *mens rea* can include recklessness. Examples of basic intent crimes include involuntary manslaughter, s.20 OAPA, s.47 OAPA, assault and battery.

If the defendant is voluntarily intoxicated, he or she will not have a defence to a crime of specific intent if he or she has been reckless. Involuntary intoxication, on the other hand, will provide a defence to basic intent crimes.

For most offences of specific intent, there is a similar basic intent crime. For example, if the defendant is charged with murder and pleads intoxication, he or she may be charged with the basic intent crime of manslaughter instead. However, not all specific intent offences have a corresponding basic intent crime, and in these cases, intoxication can be a complete defence. An example of such an offence is theft.

'Dutch courage'

If someone deliberately gets intoxicated to give himself or herself 'Dutch courage' to commit a crime, intoxication will not be a defence to any crime — even to crimes that can only be committed with a specific intention.

Burden and standard of proof

The burden of proof rests with the defendant. He or she must provide some evidence of intoxication before the defence can be put before the jury. It is then up to the prosecution to prove beyond reasonable doubt that, despite this evidence, the defendant still formed the necessary *mens rea*.

Effect

The effect of intoxication varies according to the type of crime that the defendant is charged with and whether the defendant was voluntarily or involuntarily intoxicated.

If the defendant was voluntarily intoxicated and incapable of forming *mens rea*, he or she has a defence to specific intent crimes but not crimes of basic intent. If the defendant is charged with a specific intent crime that does not have a corresponding basic intent crime, e.g. theft, intoxication can provide a complete defence.

If the defendant is involuntarily intoxicated and incapable of forming *mens rea*, he or she will have a defence to both basic and specific intent crimes.

Evaluation

Distinction between basic and specific intent crimes

It is difficult to know for certain which offences the courts will class as specific intent crimes and which they will class as basic intent crimes. This is because the general rule is not always consistently applied. Critics argue that the distinction should be abandoned and the matter left in the hands of the jury in each case.

Inconsistency in its effect

Some specific intent crimes, such as theft, do not have a corresponding basic intent crime. Intoxication therefore operates as a complete defence to those crimes. However, for specific intent crimes that *do* have a corresponding basic intent offence, the defendant will be convicted. Furthermore, there is no logical reason why some crimes have a corresponding offence while others do not.

Reform

Ensuring that all specific intent crimes have a corresponding basic intent offence

It has been suggested that the current distinction between basic and specific offences should be maintained, as long as all crimes of specific intent are given a corresponding basic intent crime.

Intoxication offence

The Butler Committee suggested that the current law should be replaced with a new offence of 'dangerous intoxication'. Juries could then find a defendant guilty of 'dangerous intoxication' rather than the offence committed.

Full defence

Critics have argued that since the defendant was incapable of forming *mens rea*, legal principle dictates that he or she should be acquitted. This would mean that intoxication would operate as a complete defence to any crime.

TOPIC 11 Duress and necessity

The defences of duress and necessity are available in situations where the defendant is forced to commit a crime in order to avoid harm to him or herself or others. Both defences are limited in their use.

A Duress

Duress is a complete defence for most crimes. The burden of proof is on the prosecution to disprove that the defendant was under duress.

However, duress is not available for the offence of murder (*R* v *Howe*, 1987), nor is it a defence for attempted murder (*R* v *Gotts*, 1991).

***R* v *Howe* (1987)**
The defendant was part of a criminal gang that tortured and killed two people. Howe was the lookout for the gang and pleaded duress to the murders. His conviction was upheld by the Court of Appeal and the House of Lords, both of which decided duress should not be available for the crime of murder. This decision overruled the previous law that allowed the defence of duress for a getaway driver who was threatened by the IRA (*DPP for Northern Ireland* v *Lynch*, 1975).

***R* v *Gotts* (1991)**
The House of Lords in *R* v *Howe* (above) also said *obiter* that duress should not be a defence for attempted murder either. The Court of Appeal and House of Lords confirmed this in *R* v *Gotts*. The defendant was threatened by his father to kill his own mother. The defendant failed to kill her but was not allowed the defence of duress as it was not an available defence for murder or attempted murder.

There are two types of duress: duress by threats and duress by circumstances.

1 *Duress by threats*

The ability to use this defence has been reduced since the case of *R* v *Hasan* (2005) — see page 101.

For the defence of duress by threats, the defendant has both the *actus reus* and *mens rea* for the crime, but conviction is escaped because his or her will is overborne by personal threats or by threats to family members or people for whom the defendant is responsible.

The test for this defence (known as the 'Graham test') is made up of two parts; the first involves a subjective element and the second an objective element. It was established by the Court of Appeal in *R* v *Graham* (1982).

***R* v *Graham* (1982)**
The defendant lived with his wife and homosexual lover. His lover threatened him into killing his wife. The Court of Appeal did not regard the threats as sufficient to constitute the defence of duress.

For duress by threats to succeed, the jury needs to consider the two key questions raised by Lord Lane CJ:

- Was the defendant impelled to act in the belief that he or she or others would be killed or physically injured if he or she did not comply with the threats?
- If so, would a sober person of reasonable firmness sharing the same characteristics of the defendant have acted in the same way?

1.1 The Graham test part 1

The first part of the Graham test requires the threats to be serious, unavoidable and imminent, and the duress must not be self-induced.

1.1a Seriousness of the threats

Threats of death and personal injury are necessary for the defence of duress.

***R* v *Valderrama-Vega* (1985)**

The defendant was caught smuggling cocaine from Columbia. He claimed he was under duress from the drug barons in Columbia who threatened to kill him and his family and to expose the defendant's homosexuality. The defendant would also face financial difficulties if he did not help smuggle the drugs. The court held that only the threats to him and his family were able to afford the defence of duress.

Threats to property would not be regarded as duress.

1.1b Unavoidable and imminent threat

The defendant must not be able to avoid the threat. This means that he or she cannot use the defence of duress if he or she has time to inform the police or to avoid the crime that he or she been threatened into committing.

***R* v *Gill* (1963)**

The threat needs to be immediate. The defence of duress was not accepted when the defendant stole his employer's lorry after being threatened, as he had had time to go to the police.

***R* v *Hasan* (2005)**

The House of Lords stated that the threat had to be immediate or almost immediate, so that the defendant did not have time to go to the police or avoid committing the crime.

See page 101 for the details of *R* v *Hasan* (2005).

The decision in *R* v *Hasan* (2005) has restricted a defendant's chance of proving the defence of duress. Previous cases such as *R* v *Hudson and Taylor* (1971) and *R* v *Abdul-Hussain* (1999), which were allowed the defence of duress, would probably fail since the case of *Hasan*. Hudson and Taylor were allowed the defence of duress for the offence of perjury when they lied in court after being threatened by one of the friends of the defendant. In *R* v *Abdul-Hussain*, Iraqi fugitives were allowed the defence of duress when they hijacked an aeroplane, which they flew to England.

It does not matter if there was no actual threat, as long as the defendant honestly *thought* that there was an imminent threat. *Hasan* stated that the mistake of the threat must be honest and reasonable.

1.1c Self-induced duress

The defence of duress is not available where the defendant has voluntarily associated with criminals. The defendant should have reasonably foreseen that he or she might be forced to commit crimes by threats or violence.

***R* v *Hasan* (2005)**
The defendant was the driver for a prostitute whose boyfriend threatened him with violence if he did not commit a burglary. The defendant was caught and tried to use the defence of duress. The House of Lords did not allow the defence, as his duress was self-induced, regardless of whether he had foreseen that he might be forced to commit crimes. All that was necessary was that either the defendant foresaw or it was reasonable to foresee that he might be forced.

1.2 The Graham test part 2

The second part of the Graham test is objective. It requires a sober person of reasonable firmness to have also done as the defendant did. The court will, however, take into account some of the defendant's characteristics.

1.2a Characteristics of the defendant

The court takes into account the age and sex of the defendant, as this may affect his or her ability to resist pressure. The jury can also take into account a defendant's physical disability or mental illness.

Self-induced characteristics, such as being a drug addict, are not taken into account (*R* v *Flatt*, 1996).

***R* v *Boden* (1996)**
The defendant was of low IQ and it was argued that this characteristic made him more susceptible to threats. The Court of Appeal did not allow this to be taken into consideration.

2 *Duress by circumstances*

Like duress by threats, this type of duress requires fear of imminent death or serious injury (*R* v *Baker and Wilkins*, 1997). It has mainly been used as a defence for driving offences, where defendants claim to have felt forced to commit a driving offence due to the circumstances that they found themselves in, rather than because they had been threatened to do so. The defence has been extended to other crimes, e.g. possession of a firearm in *R* v *Pommell* (1995) or hijacking in *R* v *Abdul-Hussain* (1999).

***R* v *Conway* (1989)**
The defendant was in his car with a passenger when two plain-clothed policemen started running towards them. Not knowing that they were policemen, the defendant and the passenger feared that they were in immediate threat of personal injury because the passenger had been recently threatened in such a way and the defendant drove off recklessly at high speed. The Court of Appeal quashed the conviction for reckless driving, as the judge should have allowed the jury to consider duress of circumstances as a possible defence at the trial.

***R* v *Martin* (1989)**
The defendant drove his stepson to work, even though he was disqualified from driving. The reason he drove while disqualified was because his wife threatened to kill herself if he did not. The Court of Appeal established a two-stage test for duress of circumstances that is similar to the Graham test. It involves a subjective test, in that the defendant reasonably believed that death or serious injury would result. The second part of the test is objective, in that the sober person of

reasonable firmness would have done as the defendant did. The defendant was successful and his conviction was quashed.

B Necessity

Dudley and Stephens did get the death penalty reduced to imprisonment for the murder.

The defence of necessity is similar to duress of circumstances and was considered not to exist until the case of *Re A* (2000). The case of *R* v *Dudley and Stephens* (1884) did not allow the defence for murder. In this case, four sailors were shipwrecked and had been floating miles from land for 20 days. They killed and ate the cabin boy, who had become unconscious. Their charge of murder was upheld and the defence of necessity (the fact that they would have died if they had not eaten the victim) was not allowed.

A later case did not allow the defence of necessity either, as Lord Denning was concerned that people would use the defence too much, e.g. if they were hungry it would be necessary for them to steal food. In *Southwalk London Borough Council* v *Williams* (1971), a family who were evicted from an empty council house could not plead the defence of necessity in that they would be homeless if they were not allowed to squat.

Re A (2000)

As this case involved the civil law, it is only persuasive on the criminal law.

The Court of Appeal established the defence of necessity when it authorised the separation of the conjoined twins Jodie and Mary. The court was involved in this case as the conjoined babies would not survive if they were not separated. It was known, however, that if they were separated, one of the babies would die. The parents of the babies did not want them to be separated but the court authorised the operation.

The test for necessity requires that an act was necessary to avoid inevitable evil, no more was done than was necessary, and the evil inflicted was not disproportionate to the evil avoided.

C Evaluation

The defence of necessity is criticised because the leading case (*Re A*, 2000) involved the civil law. Furthermore, because it is so similar to duress of circumstances, many consider that it need not be a separate defence. Lord Woolf thought that necessity and duress of circumstances were different terms for the same thing. However, the case of *Re A* (2000) does illustrate one difference — necessity is available as a defence for murder, whereas duress is not.

The case of *R* v *Hasan* (2005) wanted to restrict the use of the duress defence, so that only people who really deserve it can use it. The test for deciding if the defendant voluntarily exposed himself or herself to risk, and therefore had self-induced duress, is objective and could mean that under this defence no one can associate with a criminal on the off-chance that he or she will be threatened. Baroness Hale did not agree with the majority in the House of Lords, as she feared that victims of domestic violence would be regarded as having self-induced duress if their violent partners forced them to commit a crime. She thought that the test for whether the duress was self-induced should be subjective, in that the defendant foresaw a risk that he or she may be forced to commit a crime.

The fact that duress is not available for the offence of murder (*R* v *Howe*, 1987) and attempted murder (*R* v *Gotts*, 1991) has been criticised by the legal academics Smith and Hogan. The 1997 Law Commission report 'Defences of General Application' also argues that duress should be a defence to all crimes. In 2005, the Law Commission recommended that duress should be a defence to the proposed new crime of first-degree murder.

The objective nature of the second part of the 'Graham test' is restrictive, as it does not take into account many of the defendant's characteristics. It particularly limits any mental problems to recognised psychiatric illnesses only.

It may be better if the defence of duress were abolished and instead taken into account as a mitigating factor when the judge decides the sentence.

Summary of Topic 11

Duress

Duress is a complete defence for most crimes. The burden of proof is on the prosecution to disprove that the defendant was under duress.

Duress is not available for the offence of murder (*R* v *Howe*, 1987), nor is it a defence for attempted murder (*R* v *Gotts*, 1991).

There are two types of duress: duress by threats and duress by circumstances.

Duress by threats

For the defence of duress by threats, the defendant has both the *actus reus* and the *mens rea* for the crime, but conviction is escaped because his or her will is overborne by personal threats or by threats to family members or people for whom the defendant is responsible.

The test for this defence is made up of two parts and was established by the Court of Appeal in *R* v *Graham* (1982):

- Was the defendant impelled to act in the belief that he or she or others would be killed or physically injured if he or she did not comply with the threats?
- If so, would a sober person of reasonable firmness sharing the same characteristics of the defendant have acted in the same way?

The Graham test part 1

The first part of the Graham test requires the threats to be serious, unavoidable and imminent, and the duress must not be self-induced.

Seriousness of the threats

Threats of death and personal injury are necessary for the defence of duress (*R* v *Valderrama-Vega*, 1985).

Unavoidable and imminent threat
The defendant must not be able to avoid the threat. This means that he or she cannot use the defence of duress if he or she has time to inform the police or avoid the crime that he or she has been threatened into committing (*R* v *Gill*, 1963).

It does not matter if there was no actual threat, as long as the defendant honestly *thought* that there was an imminent threat. *Hasan* stated that the mistake of the threat must be honest and reasonable.

Self-induced duress
The defence of duress is not available where the defendant has voluntarily associated with criminals. The defendant should have reasonably foreseen that he or she might be forced to commit crimes by threats or violence, e.g. *R* v *Hasan* (2005).

The Graham test part 2
The second part of the Graham test is objective. It requires that a sober person of reasonable firmness would also have done as the defendant did. The court will, however, take into account the age and sex of the defendant, as this may affect his or her ability to resist pressure. The jury can also take into account a defendant's physical disability or mental illness (*R* v *Boden*, 1996).

Duress by circumstances
Like duress by threats, this type of duress requires fear of imminent death or serious injury (*R* v *Baker and Wilkins*, 1997). It has mainly been used as a defence for driving offences (*R* v *Conway*, 1989 and *R* v *Martin*, 1989), where defendants claim to have felt forced to commit a driving offence due to the circumstances that they found themselves in, rather than because they had been threatened to do so. The defence has been extended to other crimes, e.g. possession of a firearm in *R* v *Pommell* (1995) or hijacking in *R* v *Abdul-Hussain* (1999).

Necessity

The defence of necessity is similar to duress of circumstances and was considered not to exist until the case of *Re A* (2000). The test for necessity requires that the act was necessary to avoid inevitable evil, no more was done than was necessary, and the evil inflicted was not disproportionate to the evil avoided. In *Southwalk London Borough Council* v *Williams* (1971), a family who were evicted from an empty council house could not plead the defence of necessity in that they would be homeless if they were not allowed to squat.

Evaluation

The defence of necessity is criticised because the leading case (*Re A*, 2000) involved the civil law. Furthermore, because it is so similar to duress of circumstances, many consider that it need not be a separate defence.

The case of *R* v *Hasan* (2005) wanted to restrict the use of the duress defence so that only people who really deserve it can use it.

The fact that duress is not available for the offence of murder (*R* v *Howe*, 1987) and attempted murder (*R* v *Gotts*, 1991) has been criticised by the legal academics Smith and Hogan.

The objective nature of the second part of the Graham test is restrictive, as it does not take into account many of the defendant's characteristics.

It may be better if the defence of duress were abolished and instead taken into account as a mitigating factor when the judge decides the sentence.

TOPIC 12 Attempts

If a defendant fully intends to commit a crime but for some reason fails to complete the *actus reus*, the law on attempts is available to ensure that he or she can still be prosecuted. The rationale behind the law is that those who plan to commit an offence but fail to perform it deserve to be punished, and its existence means that if the police are aware that an offence is going to be committed, they do not have to wait until it is complete before arresting the suspect. If the defendant is found guilty, he or she will usually face the same maximum penalty that applies to the full offence.

The problem with prosecuting those who attempt crimes is where to draw the line. Should they be liable as soon as they think of committing a crime? Obviously the law does not seek to punish those who merely think about committing an offence. After all, most people have probably thought about committing a crime, but few ever would, and it would also be virtually impossible to secure a conviction in those circumstances. The difficulty is at what stage the defendant becomes criminally liable for an attempted crime.

A Actus reus

The law on attempts is contained in s.1(1) of the **Criminal Attempts Act 1981**:

> If with intent to commit an offence to which this section applies, a person does an act which is more than merely preparatory to the commission of the offence, he is guilty of attempting to commit the offence.

1 More than merely preparatory

Since the Criminal Attempts Act does not define the phrase 'more than merely preparatory', this is a matter for the jury to decide in each case, although the judge will first consider whether there is enough evidence to go before the jury. It is up to the jury to decide whether the defendant passed the preparation stage and progressed to something beyond that. Obviously, this is not an easy decision to make.

***R* v *Gullefer* (1987)**
The defendant had placed a bet on a greyhound at a racetrack, but it soon became obvious that his choice was not going to win. The defendant ran onto the track in order to disrupt the race, so that it would be declared void and he could then retrieve his stake money from the bookmakers. The question was whether his actions could be said to be more then merely preparatory to the commission of theft. The Court of Appeal overturned his conviction for attempted theft. They said that he had not gone beyond the preparatory stages, as he still had to go to ask for his money back from the bookmakers.

Previously, the law on attempts was covered by the common law, and a series of tests was developed by the courts to decide whether the defendant was guilty or not. Since *Gullefer*, the courts have stressed that the words of the **Criminal**

Attempts Act 1981 are to be followed, rather than the tests laid down in pre-statute cases.

***R* v *Geddes* (1996)**
The defendant was found in the boys' toilets of a school. He ran off, leaving a rucksack containing string, tape and a knife. He was convicted of attempted false imprisonment but on appeal this was quashed, as despite the fact that he clearly had the requisite intention, his actions were preparatory. He had not progressed beyond the preparatory stage, since he had not made contact with any of the boys. He had simply put himself in the position of being able to commit the offence and had not moved into the implementation stage.

***R* v *Tosti* (1997)**
The defendant and an accomplice had oxyacetylene equipment, which they hid in a hedge near to a barn that they planned to break into. They walked up to the barn door and examined the lock on it. When they realised that they were being watched, they ran away. On appeal, their convictions for attempted burglary were upheld, as the Court of Appeal said that there was evidence that showed they had gone beyond the preparatory stages and had actually tried to commit the offence.

Remember, whether the defendant has passed the preparatory stage is a question for the jury in each case.

2 *Attempting the impossible*

Section 1(2) of the **Criminal Attempts Act 1981** states:

> A person may be guilty of attempting to commit an offence to which this section applies even though the facts are such that the commission of the offence is impossible.

Thus, the person who puts his or her hand into an empty pocket can be found guilty of attempted theft, even though it would be impossible for him or her to be convicted of the full offence as there was nothing to steal. In this example the crime is physically impossible, but in other circumstances the crime may be legally impossible, for instance if the defendant attempts to handle what he or she thinks are stolen goods but the goods are not in fact stolen.

***Anderton* v *Ryan* (1985)**
The defendant bought a video recorder that she believed to be stolen. After confessing this to the police, they found no evidence to show that the equipment had actually been stolen but the defendant was nonetheless charged with attempting to handle stolen goods. She was convicted, but on appeal the House of Lords quashed her conviction, despite the fact that the wording of s.1(2) of the Act clearly made her guilty.

This was an unexpected result and one that was to be changed only a year later.

***R* v *Shivpuri* (1986)**
The defendant was arrested after being found carrying a suitcase that he believed contained either heroin or cannabis. In fact, the substance was merely dried cabbage leaves. The defendant was convicted of attempting to be knowingly concerned in dealing in controlled drugs. His conviction was upheld by the Court of Appeal. On appeal to the House of Lords, it took the opportunity to correct the mistake made a year earlier in *Anderton* v *Ryan*. It used the 1966

Practice Statement to depart from its previous decision. The defendant was held to be guilty, since he had clearly intended to commit the offence and had carried out an act that was more than merely preparatory to the commission of the offence.

If conviction of a crime is impossible because there is no such offence, the defendant cannot be guilty of attempting it.

***R* v *Taaffe* (1984)**
The defendant's luggage was searched by customs on arrival into the UK and a number of packages were found in his luggage. He was asked what they contained and replied that it was money. He thought that he was committing a crime by importing currency into the UK. In fact there is no such crime, so the defendant could not be guilty of attempting it. It was irrelevant that he thought he was actually committing a crime.

B *Mens rea*

1 *Intention*

In order to be liable for an attempted offence, the statute states that the defendant must act with intent to commit an offence. Therefore, the *mens rea* for an attempted offence is intention. Thus, for example, the *mens rea* for attempted murder is an intention to kill; an intention to cause GBH, which would be sufficient for a murder conviction, will not be enough to make the defendant liable for attempted murder.

***R* v *Mohan* (1976)**
The defendant refused to stop when a police officer signalled for him to do so. Instead, he drove towards the officer, who managed to move out of the way in time. The defendant's conviction for attempted GBH was quashed due to an error by the trial judge. The Court of Appeal stated that the *mens rea* for an attempted offence was satisfied by a decision to bring about the commission of the offence — in other words, only intention would suffice.

Always include examples to enhance your answer.

2 *Conditional intent*

A conditional intent may arise if, for example in the offence of theft, instead of having a specific object in mind the defendant intends to take anything worth stealing. This may be enough to make him or her liable for an attempted offence.

***R* v *Husseyn* (1977)**
The defendant and another man were seen standing by the back of a van containing diving equipment. They had intended to take anything worth stealing but ran off when the police approached them. The defendant was convicted of attempting to steal the diving equipment but this was quashed on appeal — he

had been charged specifically with attempting to steal the diving equipment when, in fact, his true intention was to steal anything.

This case appeared to leave a gap in the law, which posed a problem for the courts. A defendant could simply claim that he or she was not intending to steal whatever specific object was detailed in the charge, and, following *Husseyn*, he or she would be acquitted. The problem was resolved in the following case.

***Attorney General's References (Nos. 1 and 2)* (1979)**
The Court of Appeal held that a conditional intent was enough to impose liability for an attempted offence if the charge does not refer to specific items. In *Husseyn*, the defendant could have been found guilty if he had been charged with attempted theft of anything from the van instead of being charged specifically with attempted theft of the diving equipment, as there was no evidence that this was his intention.

C Evaluation

1 *Sentence*

Some people argue that a person convicted of an attempted offence should not face the same maximum penalty as someone who has actually committed the full offence, since he or she is not as blameworthy. Those in favour of the current system argue that often a person will only fail to commit the full offence because he or she is caught beforehand or because something beyond his or her control occurs to prevent him or her. They claim that if the defendant intended to commit the crime then he or she is as blameworthy as the defendant who actually committed it, and should therefore face the same sentence.

2 *Determining when an act is 'more than merely preparatory'*

As the statute gives no definition of what is meant by the phrase 'more than merely preparatory', it is left to juries and appeal courts to decide. This creates uncertainty and can allow defendants who are clearly a danger to avoid liability, as in *Geddes*.

3 *No opportunity to withdraw*

Once the defendant has performed an act that is more than merely preparatory, there is no opportunity or incentive for him or her to withdraw, since he or she will be liable for the attempted offence. As this carries the same maximum penalty as the full offence, he or she might as well continue, since there is nothing to be gained by withdrawal.

Summary of Topic 12

Actus reus

The law on attempts is contained in s.1(1) of the **Criminal Attempts Act 1981**:

> If with intent to commit an offence to which this section applies, a person does an act which is more than merely preparatory to the commission of the offence, he is guilty of attempting to commit the offence.

The defendant must perform an act that is 'more than merely preparatory' to the commission of the offence. Since the Criminal Attempts Act does not define the phrase 'more than merely preparatory', this is a matter for the jury to decide in each case, although the judge will first consider whether there is enough evidence to go before the jury. It is up to the jury to decide whether the defendant has passed the preparation stage and progressed to something beyond that. Obviously, this is not an easy decision to make.

Previously, the law on attempts was covered by the common law, and a series of tests was developed by the courts to decide whether the defendant was guilty or not. Now the courts have stressed that the words of the **Criminal Attempts Act 1981** are to be followed, rather than the old tests.

Section 1(2) of the **Criminal Attempts Act 1981** ensures that the defendant may be found guilty of attempting to commit an offence, even though the facts are such that the commission of the offence is impossible.

Mens rea

In order to be liable for an attempted offence, the statute states that the defendant must act with intent to commit an offence. Therefore the *mens rea* for an attempted offence is intention. Thus, for example, the *mens rea* for attempted murder is an intention to kill; an intention to cause GBH, which would be sufficient for a murder conviction, will not be enough to make the defendant liable for attempted murder.

A conditional intent may arise if, for example in the offence of theft, instead of having a specific object in mind, the defendant intends to take anything worth stealing. This may be enough to make him or her liable for an attempted offence.

Evaluation

Sentence

Some people argue that the person convicted of an attempted offence should not face the same maximum penalty as someone who has actually committed the full offence, since he or she is not as blameworthy.

Determining when an act is 'more than merely preparatory'

As the statute gives no definition of what is meant by the phrase 'more than merely preparatory', it is left to juries and appeal courts to decide. This creates uncertainty.

No opportunity to withdraw

Once the defendant has performed an act that is more than merely preparatory, there is no opportunity or incentive for him or her to withdraw, since he or she will be liable for the attempted offence. As this carries the same maximum penalty as the full offence, he or she might as well continue, since there is nothing to be gained by withdrawal.

TOPIC 13 Theft

Theft is an offence triable either way, with a maximum sentence of 7 years' imprisonment.

Theft is defined in s.1 of the **Theft Act 1968**:

> A person is guilty of theft if he dishonestly appropriates property belonging to another with the intention of permanently depriving the other of it.

A Actus reus

1 Appropriation

Appropriation is defined in s.3 of the **Theft Act 1968**:

> (1) Any assumption by a person of the rights of an owner amounts to appropriation, and this includes, where he has come by the property (innocently or not) without stealing it, any later assumption of a right to it by keeping or dealing with it as owner.
>
> (2) Where property or a right or interest in property is or purports to be transferred for value to a person acting in good faith, no later assumption by him of rights which he believed himself to be acquiring shall, by reason of any defect in the transferor's title, amount to theft of the property.

Section 3(2) provides a defence to people who buy stolen goods in good faith.

Appropriation includes assuming any rights of the owner, e.g. touching, moving, selling, destroying etc.

The case of *Morris* also stated that the appropriation has to be without the owner's consent. However, this part of the judgement has been overruled in the cases of *Lawrence* and *Gomez* (see below).

***R* v *Morris* (1983)**
The defendant's assumption of any one right of the owner is sufficient to constitute appropriation. This means that touching someone's property is an appropriation, yet it is not theft unless the other elements defined in s.1 are present as well.

In this case, changing the price of an item in a supermarket to that of a lower-priced item was considered to be appropriation.

An appropriation can take place even with the consent of the victim.

***Lawrence* v *Metropolitan Police Commissioner* (1972)**
An Italian student who spoke little English got into a taxi in London. The student showed the defendant (the taxi driver) an address written down. At the end of the journey the fare was 52p, and the victim offered the taxi driver £1. The driver stated it was not enough, so the victim opened his wallet and the defendant took out another £6 with the victim's permission. The House of Lords unanimously decided that this amounted to theft, despite the victim's consent.

***R* v *Gomez* (1993)**
The defendant worked in an electrical goods shop. He convinced the manager to sell £17,000 of goods to his accomplice. The goods were paid for using cheques known by Gomez to be worthless. The House of Lords followed the decision in *Lawrence v Metropolitan Police Commissioner* (1972) and confirmed that an appropriation can take place with the owner's consent.

***R* v *Hinks* (2000)**
The defendant befriended a rich man of low intelligence. She convinced him to withdraw £300 a day and put it into her bank account. The majority of the

House of Lords held that the £60,000 she had received from the victim was an appropriation, regardless of it being a gift. The defendant's charge of theft was upheld.

2 *Property*

'Property' is defined in the **Theft Act 1968**:

- Section 4(1) states that property includes money and all other property, real or personal, including things in action and other intangible property.
- Section 4(2) states that a person cannot steal land or things forming part of land and severed from it by him or by his direction.
- Section 4(3) provides that mushrooms, flowers, fruit and foliage growing wild cannot be stolen unless they are taken for reward or for sale or other commercial purpose.
- Section 4(4) states that wild animals cannot be stolen unless they have been tamed or are normally kept in captivity.

2.1 Real property

Real property means land and is referred to in s.4(2). There are, however, three exceptions:

- when someone is trusted to sell or dispose of the land or anything on it and he or she breaches that confidence (e.g. the trustee benefits from the sale of the land)
- when someone appropriates from land anything by severing, causing it to be severed or taking it after it has been severed (this includes taking crops, soil, bricks etc. from another person's property)
- when a tenant takes something from land that is let to him or her (e.g. if a person who is renting a house takes some of the furniture when he or she moves out)

2.2 Personal property

This is the most usual type of 'other property'. It includes physical objects such as a stereo.

***R* v *Kelly and Lindsay* (1998)**

The defendants took body parts from the Royal College of Surgeons. They were found guilty of theft, even though body parts are not usually regarded as property.

Electricity is not property but it is a crime to make dishonest use of it, to waste it or to divert it (s.13 of the **Theft Act 1968**).

2.3 Things in action and other intangible property

This is property that does not exist physically but gives the owner legal rights. It includes money in a bank account, debts, shares and intellectual property such as copyright.

***Oxford* v *Moss* (1979)**

A student who took an exam paper, read the questions and then returned it could not be charged with theft of the information on the paper. This is because confidential information is not regarded as property. If he had kept the exam paper, this would have been theft of the paper itself. This happened in *R* v *Akbar* (2002), when a teacher was convicted of theft when she took exam papers and gave them to her students.

3 *Belonging to another*

'Belonging to another' is defined in s.5(1) of the **Theft Act 1968**:

> Property shall be regarded as belonging to any person having possession or control over it, or having any proprietary right or interest.

'Proprietary right or interest' means ownership. The defendant must be charged with the theft of the property from the actual owner.

***R* v *Dyke and Munro* (2002)**
The defendants collected and kept money intended for a children's cancer fund. They were charged with stealing money from the public who had put the money in the tins. The Court of Appeal quashed their conviction. It said that the defendants should not have been charged with stealing the money from the unknown members of the public who put it into the collection tin. Instead, they should have been charged with stealing the money from the charity, as ownership of the money had passed to the charity when it had been put in the collection tin.

***Powell* v *McRae* (1977)**
The defendant worked on the turnstiles at Wembley Stadium and allowed a person without a ticket entry for £2. He was found not guilty of theft, as this money did not belong to his employer.

The decision in *Powell* v *McRae* may no longer stand, as the Privy Council thought that an employee who makes an illegal profit from his or her job should be liable for theft (*Attorney General for Hong Kong* v *Reid*, 1993).

***R* v *Marshall, Coombes and Eren* (1998)**
The defendants took 1-day London Underground tickets from passengers who had no further use for them and sold them on to other passengers. The Court of Appeal upheld their convictions for theft, as the tickets remained the property of London Underground, regardless that the passengers who had originally bought them had willingly given them to the defendants.

Abandonment may also affect the defendant's *mens rea* (see *R* v *Small* on page 116).

Property is still owned, even if it has been lost and the owner is no longer trying to find it. Ownerless property, however, cannot be stolen. The courts are keen to ensure that the property has been completely abandoned before they allow it to be regarded as ownerless.

***R* v *Rostron* (2003)**
The defendant retrieved golf balls from the lake on a golf course. His conviction was upheld by the Court of Appeal, which stated that it is a question of fact for the jury to decide if the golf club had abandoned the balls or if it still owned them.

A person may be guilty when stealing his or her own property.

***R* v *Turner (No. 2)* (1971)**
The defendant took his own car from a garage that had repaired it, without paying for the repairs. He was found guilty of theft, as the garage had possession of the car, which amounted to a proprietary interest.

4 *Obligation to use property in a particular way*

'Obligation to use property in a particular way' is defined in s.5(3) of the **Theft Act 1968**:

> Where a person received property from or on account of another, and is under an obligation to the other to retain and deal with the property or its proceeds in a particular way, the property or proceeds shall be regarded (as against him) as belonging to the other.

This subsection is designed to cover situations where money is given to someone for a particular purpose. Even though ownership of the property has passed to the defendant, it will be regarded as theft if the defendant uses it for some other purpose. An example of this is where money is being held in trust.

***R* v *Hall* (1972)**
Section 5(3) did not apply in this case. The defendant was a travel agent who had taken deposits from customers when they booked a holiday. The travel agent went out of business and was unable to book the holidays, but was found not guilty of theft. The deposits were not given to the defendant for the purpose of booking a holiday; they were given as security for the booking. There was no obligation to use the deposit money to book the holiday.

***R* v *Wain* (1995)**
The defendant raised money for a 'telethon'. He deposited £3,000 into a bank account and was then allowed by the organisers to transfer it to his own account so that he could write a cheque for the money. However, the defendant then spent it. Even though he had put the money in his own bank account, the Court of Appeal decided that the money still belonged to the telethon organisers, as they had given it to him with an obligation to deal with it in a particular way according to s.5(3).

5 *Property acquired by mistake*

'Property acquired by mistake' is defined in s.5(4) of the **Theft Act 1968**:

> Where a person gets property by another's mistake, and is under an obligation to make restoration...an intention not to make restoration shall be regarded accordingly as an intention to deprive that person of the property or proceeds.

If someone receives property by mistake and then does not give it back, this can amount to theft. A legal obligation to pay it back is therefore required, rather than just a moral obligation because it is the right thing to do.

***Attorney General's Reference (No. 1 of 1983)* (1985)**
The defendant was overpaid by her employers. The Court of Appeal decided that she was legally obliged to return the excess money under s.5(4), even though she had taken ownership of the money when it was paid into her bank account.

***R* v *Gilks* (1972)**
There was no legal obligation for the defendant to pay back money that he was given by mistake in a betting shop.

B Mens rea

The *mens rea* of theft requires the defendant to be dishonest and to have the intention to permanently deprive the owner of the property.

1 Dishonesty

An example of s.2(1)(a) would be if you took something that you thought was yours. An example of s.2(1)(b) would be if you borrowed something you thought the owner would let you borrow. An example of s.2(1)(c) would be if you found 10p in the street.

The **Theft Act 1968** does not define the word 'dishonesty', but it does give some guidance in s.2(1) as to what would not be considered dishonest. According to this section, a person's appropriation of property belonging to another is not to be regarded as dishonest if he or she appropriates the property in the belief that:

- he or she has in law the right to deprive the other of it, on behalf of himself or herself or a third person
- he or she would have the other's consent if the other knew of the appropriation and the circumstances of it
- the person to whom the property belongs cannot be discovered by taking reasonable steps

***R* v *Small* (1988)**

This case concerned s.2(1)(c). The defendant took a car that he thought had been abandoned. There was much evidence of this, in that it had been left in the same place for 2 weeks with its doors unlocked and the keys in the ignition. The car had a flat battery, no petrol and a flat tyre. The Court of Appeal quashed the defendant's conviction for theft, as it was up to the jury to decide if the defendant believed that the owner could not be found after he had taken reasonable steps.

The Court of Appeal established a two-stage test for dishonesty in *R* v *Ghosh* (1982). It combines both an objective and subjective element. The jury has to answer the following questions:

- Has the defendant been dishonest by the ordinary standards of reasonable and honest people?
- If the answer is yes to the first question, the court should ask whether the defendant realised that he or she was dishonest by those standards. If the answer is yes to the second question, there is dishonesty.

According to the **Theft Act 1968**, a defendant's willingness to pay does not necessarily mean that he or she was not dishonest. This is mentioned in s.2(2): 'Willingness to pay does not prevent a finding of dishonesty.'

2 Intention to permanently deprive

'Intention to permanently deprive' is defined in s.6(1) of the **Theft Act 1968**:

> A person appropriating property belonging to another without meaning the other permanently to lose the thing itself is nevertheless to be regarded as having the intention of permanently depriving the other of it if his intention is to treat the thing as his own to dispose of regardless of the other's rights; and a borrowing or lending of it may amount to so treating it if, but only if, the borrowing or lending is for a period and in circumstances making it equivalent to an outright taking or disposal.

***R* v *Velumyl* (1989)**
A company director took money from the safe with the intention of paying it back. He was found guilty of theft because he would not return the exact money that he took. Instead, he would replace it with different money of the same value. He was not entitled to take the money and it did not matter that he was going to pay it back.

***R* v *Lloyd and Others* (1985)**
The defendant worked at a cinema. He gave the films to his friends to copy and then returned them straightaway. There was no theft because the films had not reduced in value, they were not in a changed state, and the defendant did not intend to permanently deprive the owner of them.

C Evaluation

Many of the advantages and disadvantages of theft are often regarded as complicated. The Law Commission Report 2002 and Professor Griew's 1985 article entitled 'Dishonesty' contain many of the arguments surrounding this area of law.

The fact that theft is defined in an Act of Parliament (**Theft Act 1968**) means that it is the job of judges to interpret the wording. The Act is worded specifically and is often described as a technical law. This means that people can be found guilty or not guilty of theft on a technicality due to the wording, rather than what would be regarded as fair. It is possible to put forward arguments that would support finding the opposite verdict in all the cases mentioned in this topic.

1 *Appropriation*

The wide interpretation of the term 'appropriation' means that the defendant only needs to assume one of the rights of the owner and not all of them. This is why Morris was convicted for changing the price labels in a shop. The interpretation also allows the courts to convict shoplifters of theft before they have even left the shop. In addition, it means that Lawrence, Gomez and Hinks could all be convicted of theft, even though the victims consented to the appropriation.

It seems that the application of the term 'appropriation' allows the courts to get a conviction easily. It could be argued that the wide interpretation makes it too easy, and is therefore unfair. It is worth remembering that all of the elements of theft need to be established. Just because someone has appropriated something does not automatically mean that he or she is guilty of theft.

2 *Property*

Property is defined in s.4(1) of the **Theft Act 1968**, yet the Act does provide some exceptions. These include land and confidential information. This led to a student being found not guilty of theft of the contents of an exam paper in *Oxford* v *Moss* (1979). The courts were also willing to stretch the existing law that states that body parts are not property. There are good reasons why body parts are not regarded as property, as it means that it is illegal to sell them. However, in *R* v *Kelly and Lindsay* (1998) this rule was ignored in order to secure a conviction.

3 *Belonging to another*

In *R* v *Dyke and Munro* (2002), the defendants were released due to a technicality concerning to whom the collection money belonged. The trial judge said that it was acceptable to convict if property belonged to persons unknown (the people who put money in the charity collection box). However, the Court of Appeal said that the money belonged to the charity.

The fact that people are capable of stealing their own property can also be evaluated. It seems unfair in theory, but the case of *R* v *Turner (No. 2)* (1971) offers a situation that may justify this rule.

The rule that property obtained by mistake is theft if there is a legal obligation to return it is defined in s.5(4). This happened in *Attorney General's Reference (No. 1 of 1983)* (1985), and it is justifiable that the defendant should have returned the money. The case of *R* v *Gilks* (1972) is harder to justify, as it seems that a gap in the law (gambling contracts are not legally enforceable) means that the defendant was not required to pay back the money he was given by mistake.

4 *Dishonesty*

The case of *R* v *Ghosh* has led to a massive amount of criticism. Professor Griew in particular has identified many problems with the two-part test.

4.1 Reasonable and honest people

The first part of the test asks the jury/magistrates to decide according to an objective test. Was the defendant dishonest according to the ordinary standards of reasonable and honest people? This means that the jury/magistrates must make a moral judgement based on honest people. These 'honest people' may differ according to the standards of the jury/magistrates personally or the circumstances of a case, e.g. a jury might not think it is completely dishonest to steal from a betting shop.

Judges may also differ in their opinion of the view of 'honest people'. In *Sinclair* v *Neighbour* (1967), the trial judge thought a manager of a shop who took £15 from the till and left an IOU note was not dishonest, whereas the Court of Appeal said that he was.

4.2 The Ghosh test is complicated

Professor Griew argued that juries might find the Ghosh test too complicated. This would lead to longer, and therefore more expensive, trials. It would also mean that the defendant might plead not guilty and opt for a jury trial, in the hope that the jury is not very honest or that it does not understand the test.

4.3 Lack of guidance

Professor Griew attributes some of the problems with dishonesty to the fact that it is left to the jury, and therefore there is a lack of precedents that state what is, and what is not, dishonest. If it were up to the judge to decide what would amount to dishonesty, there would be some case law to give guidance.

4.4 The subjective part of the test

This second part of the test is supposed to allow people to be found not guilty when they make an honest mistake. Professor Griew believes that it further confuses the jury, leading to more appeals and requiring additional evidence.

5 *Intention to permanently deprive*

Both *R* v *Velumyl* (1989) and *R* v *Lloyd and Others* (1985) can be evaluated. It seems that Velumyl was convicted on a technicality and Lloyd was acquitted on a technicality. Although Velumyl should not have been allowed to get away with taking money from the office safe, the court had to use its imagination to come up with the fact that it would not be exactly the same money that would be returned, even though it would be exactly the same amount. Lloyd, on the other hand, was able to escape charges for theft because the court did not think he had kept the films long enough.

Summary of Topic 13

Theft is defined in s.1 of the **Theft Act 1968**:

> A person is guilty of theft if he dishonestly appropriates property belonging to another with the intention of permanently depriving the other of it.

Actus reus

Appropriation

Appropriation is defined in s.3 of the **Theft Act 1968**:

> Any assumption by a person of the rights of an owner amounts to appropriation, and this includes, where he has come by the property (innocently or not) without stealing it, any later assumption of a right to it by keeping or dealing with it as owner.

The assumption of any one right of an owner is sufficient to constitute appropriation (*R* v *Morris*, 1984).

Property

Property is defined in s.4 of the **Theft Act 1968**:

> Property includes money and all other property, real or personal, including things in action and other intangible property.

Intangible property might include money in a bank account, debts, shares and intellectual property such as copyright.

Belonging to another

'Belonging to another' is defined in s.5(1) of the **Theft Act 1968**:

> Property shall be regarded as belonging to any person having possession or control over it, or having any proprietary right or interest.

'Proprietary right or interest' means ownership. The defendant must be charged with the theft of the property from the actual owner (*R* v *Dyke and Munro*, 2002). Property is still owned, even if it has been lost and the owner is no longer trying to find it (*R* v *Rostron*, 2003).

A person may be guilty when stealing his or her own property (*R* v *Turner (No. 2)*, 1971).

Obligation to use property in a particular way

Section 5(3) defines an obligation to use property in a particular way. It is regarded as theft if the property is not used in this way (*R* v *Wain*, 1995).

Property acquired by mistake

Property acquired by mistake is defined in s.5(4). It must be returned if there is a legal obligation *(Attorney General's Reference (No. 1 of 1983)*, 1985 and *R* v *Gilks*, 1972).

Mens rea

The *mens rea* of theft requires the defendant to be dishonest and to have the intention to permanently deprive the owner of the property.

Dishonesty

The **Theft Act 1968** does not define the word 'dishonesty', but it does give some guidance in s.2(1) as to what would not be considered dishonest. According to this section, a person's appropriation of property belonging to another is not to be regarded as dishonest if he or she appropriates the property in the belief that:

- he or she has in law the right to deprive the other of it, on behalf of himself or herself or a third person
- he or she would have the other's consent if the other knew of the appropriation and the circumstances of it
- the person to whom the property belongs cannot be discovered by taking reasonable steps

The Court of Appeal established a two-stage test for dishonesty in *R* v *Ghosh* (1982). This combines both an objective and a subjective element. The jury has to answer the following questions:

- Has the defendant been dishonest by the ordinary standards of reasonable and honest people?
- If the answer is yes to the first question, the court should ask whether the defendant realised that he or she was dishonest by those standards. If the answer is yes to the second question, there is dishonesty.

According to the **Theft Act 1968** s.2(2), a defendant's willingness to pay does not necessarily mean that he or she was not dishonest.

Intention to permanently deprive

Section 6(1) of the **Theft Act 1968** states:

> A person appropriating property belonging to another without meaning the other permanently to lose the thing itself is nevertheless to be regarded as having the intention of permanently depriving the other of it.

In *R* v *Velumyl* (1989), the defendant was found guilty for taking money from a safe, which he was going to replace. In *R* v *Lloyd and Others* (1985), the defendant was not guilty when he took films from a cinema and copied them.

Evaluation

Appropriation

The wide interpretation of the term 'appropriation' means that the defendant only needs to assume one of the rights of the owner and not all of them. This is why Morris was convicted for changing the price labels in a shop.

Property

Property is defined in s.4(1) of the **Theft Act 1968**, yet it does provide some exceptions. These include land and confidential information.

Belonging to another

In *R* v *Dyke and Munro* (2002), the defendants were released due to a technicality concerning to whom the collection money belonged. The trial judge said that it was acceptable to convict if property belonged to persons unknown (the people who put money in the charity collection box). However, the Court of Appeal said that the money belonged to the charity.

The fact that people are capable of stealing their own property can also be evaluated. It seems unfair in theory, but the case of *R* v *Turner* (No. 2) (1971) offers a situation that may justify this rule.

Dishonesty

The case of *R* v *Ghosh* has led to a massive amount of criticism.

Reasonable and honest people

The first part of the two-stage test for dishonesty asks the jury/magistrates to decide according to an objective test. This means that the jury/magistrates must make a moral judgement based on honest people. These 'honest people' may differ according to the standards of the jury/magistrates personally or the circumstances of a case.

The Ghosh test is complicated

Juries might find the Ghosh test too complicated. This will lead to longer, and therefore more expensive, trials.

Lack of guidance

There is a lack of any precedents that state what is, and what is not, dishonest.

The subjective part of the test

Professor Griew believes that the second part of the test for dishonesty further confuses the jury, leading to more appeals and requiring additional evidence.

Intention to permanently deprive

It seems that Velumyl was convicted on a technicality and Lloyd was acquitted on a technicality.

TOPIC 14 Burglary

Burglary is defined in the **Theft Act 1968**. According to s.9(1), a person is guilty of burglary if:

(a) he or she enters any building or part of a building as a trespasser and with intent to commit any such offence as mentioned in s.9(2) (stealing, inflicting grievous bodily harm or causing criminal damage)

or

(b) having entered any building or part of a building as a trespasser, he or she steals or attempts to steal anything in the building or that part of it or inflicts or attempts to inflict on any person therein any grievous bodily harm

Sections 9(1)(a) and 9(1)(b) cover different situations:

- Section 9(1)(a) involves entering premises with intent to commit one of the ulterior offences mentioned in s.9(2). This type of burglary is committed at the time of entry.
- Section 9(1)(b) is the same as s.9(1)(a) but requires that the defendant actually carries out the *actus reus* of either GBH, attempted GBH, theft or attempted theft.

Section 9(2) used to include rape as an ulterior offence, but this was removed by the **Sexual Offences Act 2003**.

A Actus reus

1 The meaning of 'entry'

***R* v *Collins* (1973)**

The defendant saw an open bedroom window. He climbed up a ladder and saw a naked girl lying asleep on the bed. He went back down the ladder and took off all of his clothes except for his socks. He then climbed back up and stood on the windowsill. The girl awoke and, thinking that Collins was her boyfriend, invited him in. They had sex, after which the girl realised he was not her boyfriend and told him to leave. He was charged with s.9(1)(a) but there was a misdirection at the trial and the Court of Appeal quashed his conviction.

The Court of Appeal stated that entry of the building as a trespasser had to be 'substantial and effective'. The fact that the defendant was standing on the windowsill meant that his entry was not substantial and effective. When he actually entered the bedroom he was not a trespasser, as the girl had invited him in.

***R* v *Brown* (1985)**

The defendant was charged with s.9(1)(a). He was caught with the top half of his body through a broken shop window and his feet on the ground outside. He argued that he could not be said to have entered the building, as only part of his body had been inside it. However, the Court of Appeal upheld his conviction, saying that the critical issue was whether the entry had been effective, not substantial and effective as stated in *Collins*.

It seems that, since the cases of *Brown* and *Ryan*, the entry need be neither effective nor substantial.

***R* v *Ryan* (1996)**

The defendant was found trapped in a downstairs window, with only his head and right arm inside the building, and had to be freed by the fire brigade. He was convicted of burglary and appealed on the grounds that his entry had not been effective as he was unable to steal anything on account of being stuck. The Court of Appeal upheld his conviction under s.9(1)(a), stating that it did not matter whether he could steal anything or not.

2 The definition of 'building'

2.1 Building

A dwelling is a residential building.

Although this definition states that vehicles and vessels are included, it does not define the word 'building'.

A tent is not a 'building'.

The type of building that is burgled affects the length of the sentence that the defendant will receive. Burglary of a dwelling carries a maximum penalty of 14 years' imprisonment, whereas the burglary of a non-dwelling carries a maximum of 10 years' imprisonment. 'Building' is discussed in s.9(4) of the **Theft Act 1968**:

> References in subsections (1) and (2) above to a building...shall also apply to an inhabited vehicle or vessel, and shall apply to any such vehicle or vessel at times when the person having a habitation in it is not there as well as at times when he is.

***Stevens* v *Gourley* (1859)**
Judge Byles defined a building as 'a structure of considerable size and intended to be permanent or at least endure for a considerable time'.

***Norfolk Constabulary* v *Seeking and Gould* (1986)**
A supermarket was using two lorry trailers as storage. Both were locked and connected to an electricity supply. The defendants were not guilty of burglary, as the containers had wheels and were, therefore, uninhabited vehicles, even though they had been used for storage for over a year.

***B and S* v *Leathley* (1979)**
A storage container that had been used as a freezer on a farm for over 2 years was classed as a building. It was resting on railway sleepers with its wheels removed, it had a locking door and was connected to an electricity supply.

2.2 Part of a building

***R* v *Walkington* (1979)**
The defendant went into a department store. He went behind the till to look in an open cash register. When he saw that there was nothing in it he closed the drawer. The defendant was charged with burglary under s.9(1)(a). His conviction was upheld, as the Court of Appeal believed that what constitutes 'part of a building' is a question of fact for the jury to decide.

3 The requirement of a tresspass

If the defendant has permission to enter a building or part of a building, he or she is not a trespasser (see *R* v *Collins* above). However, the defendant will be a trespasser if he or she goes beyond the permission given to him or her.

***R* v *Jones and Smith* (1976)**
The defendant had permission to enter his parents' house, but when he did so in the middle of the night with his friend and took two television sets, the court held that he was a trespasser. The Court of Appeal said: 'A person is a trespasser if he

enters premises of another knowing that he is entering in excess of the permission that has been given to him to enter, or being reckless whether he is in excess of that permission.'

B *Mens rea*

The defendant must either intend or be reckless that he or she is a trespasser. In order to have the *mens rea* for s.9(1)(a), he or she must intend to commit one of the ulterior offences in s.9(2) — causing criminal damage, stealing or inflicting grievous bodily harm.

Section 9(1)(b) requires that the defendant have the required *mens rea* for the offence when he or she commits it or attempts to commit it. He or she need not have the *mens rea* for the offence at the time of entry.

1 *Conditional intent*

Attorney General's Reference Nos.1 and 2 of 1979
The defendant will still be guilty of burglary if he or she enters a building or part of a building with the intent to steal only if there is something worth stealing.

C Evaluation

1 *The meaning of 'entry'*

The development of the interpretation of the word 'enters' in both s.9(1)(a) and s.9(1)(b) has substantially widened the definition in a way that makes it easier to convict for burglary. The case of *Collins* required the entry to be 'substantial and effective'. This has, however, been subject to reinterpretation in *Brown* and *Ryan*. The judge in *Brown* decided that the entry need only be effective, i.e. the defendant was able to steal even though his whole body had not made a complete entry (Brown stuck his arm through a broken shop window).

The interpretation of entry went further in *Ryan*. The court decided that the entry did not need to be effective in that the defendant was able to carry out the ulterior offence. The entry need only be effective in that he or she managed to get into the building or part of the building (Ryan was convicted of burglary when he got his arm and head stuck through the window of a house).

This wide interpretation of the word 'enters' makes it much simpler for the prosecution to prove this part of the definition of burglary. However, burglary is a serious criminal offence, which can result in imprisonment for up to 14 years, so maybe it should require the defendant to do more than just enter the building partially.

2 The requirement of a trespass

The development of the interpretation of the word 'trespasser' in both s.9(1)(a) and s.9(1)(b) has caused much legal discussion. The case of *Collins* rested on the issue of whether the defendant entered as a trespasser. The court was only concerned with exactly where Collins was standing when the girl invited him into the house. The whole case rested on whether he was on the outside window ledge or had stepped onto the inside window ledge. It seems that this relatively small point was the main issue in deciding if Collins was guilty or not. The evidence required to establish this was lacking, as only the defendant and the girl were present, it was dark and the girl was drunk. The Court of Appeal believed that Collins was outside the window and, therefore, he was not guilty.

The Court of Appeal in *Collins* also tried to interpret the word 'trespass'. Trespassing has always been an element of the civil law, requiring intentional, reckless or negligent entry into a building without the consent of the occupier (as defined in *Archbold*). It is, however, considered inappropriate to use civil law definitions in the criminal law. Professor Smith argued that the *mens rea* of trespassing should not include civil words such as 'negligent'. Instead, it should use 'intention' or 'reckless' in a criminal sense. Professor Griew went further with his definition of the *mens rea* of a trespasser. He argued that the defendant personally must intend or at least see a risk that he or she is a trespasser, thus making the definition subjective. The Court of Appeal in *Collins* favoured Professor Griew's definition, meaning that 'trespasser' is defined as a criminal term rather than a civil term.

3 Ulterior offences

It is confusing for the average person/juror that burglary can be committed even when the defendant does not steal or even attempt to steal. Section 9(1)(a) requires the defendant only to intend to commit either theft, criminal damage of grievous bodily harm (these are known as the ulterior offences and are defined in s.9(2)). It does not seem right that someone who goes round to the victim's house intending to beat them up and cause GBH should be charged with burglary, when the common conception of the word is an offence where people break into houses and commit theft.

The ulterior offences have been modernised slightly. Before the **Sexual Offences Act 2003**, the intention to commit rape was an ulterior offence and would result in a conviction for burglary (this can be seen in the case of *Collins*). It was considered that it was more appropriate for this type of rape to be removed from the **Theft Act 1968** and put instead into the **Sexual Offences Act 2003**.

4 The definition of 'building'

The **Theft Act 1968** does not actually define 'building'. It does, however, give some examples of 'vehicles and vessels' in s.9(4). This means that the word 'building' also includes caravans and houseboats.

Judges still use the common-law definition from *Stevens* v *Gourley* (1859). Judge Byles defined a building as 'a structure of considerable size and intended to be permanent or at least endure for a considerable time'. This definition is helpful, but has been subject to legal argument in some modern cases. *B and S* v *Leathley* (1979) and *Norfolk Constabulary* v *Seeking and Gould* (1986) both rested on whether the courts considered trailers that were being used as storage containers to be buildings. The distinction was made by the courts that a container that has wheels attached is *not* a building (*Norfolk Constabulary* v *Seeking and Gould*), whereas a container that has had its wheels removed *is* a building (*B and S* v *Leathley*). This is yet another example of how technical the definition of burglary is.

Summary of Topic 14

Burglary is defined in the **Theft Act 1968**. According to s.9(1), a person is guilty of burglary if:

(a) he or she enters any building or part of a building as a trespasser and with intent to commit any such offence as mentioned in s.9(2) (stealing, inflicting grievous bodily harm or causing criminal damage)

or

(b) having entered any building or part of a building as a trespasser, he or she steals or attempts to steal anything in the building or that part of it or inflicts or attempts to inflict on any person therein any grievous bodily harm

Actus reus

The meaning of 'entry'

It seems that, since the cases of *Brown* and *Ryan*, the entry need be neither effective nor substantial .

The definition of 'building'

The type of building that is burgled affects the length of the sentence that the defendant will receive. Burglary of a dwelling carries a maximum penalty of 14 years' imprisonment, whereas the burglary of a non-dwelling carries a maximum of 10 years' imprisonment.

Building

'Building' is discussed in s.9(4) of the **Theft Act 1968**:

> References in subsections (1) and (2) above to a building...shall also apply to an inhabited vehicle or vessel, and shall apply to any such vehicle or vessel at times when the person having a habitation in it is not there as well as at times when he is.

The following cases are important in defining 'building':

- *Stevens* v *Gourley* (1859): 'a structure of considerable size and intended to be permanent or at least endure for a considerable time.'
- *Norfolk Constabulary* v *Seeking and Gould* (1986) — the containers were not a building.
- *B and S* v *Leathley* (1979) — the containers were a building.

Part of a building

R v *Walkington* (1979): the defendant went behind the till in a department store. He was charged with burglary under s.9(1)(a). His conviction was upheld as the Court of Appeal believed that what constitutes 'part of a building' is a question of fact for the jury to decide.

The requirement of a tresspass

If the defendant has permission to enter a building or part of a building, he or she is not a trespasser (*R* v *Collins*, 1973). However, the defendant *will* be a trespasser if he or she goes beyond the permission given to him or her.

In *R* v *Jones and Smith* (1976), the Court of Appeal said: 'A person is a trespasser if he enters premises of another knowing that he is entering in excess of the permission that has been given to him to enter, or being reckless whether he is in excess of that permission.'

Mens rea

- The defendant must either intend or be reckless that he or she is a trespasser.
- In order to have the *mens rea* for s.9(1)(a), the defendant must intend to commit one of the ulterior offences in s.9(2) — causing criminal damage, stealing or inflicting grievous bodily harm.
- Section 9(1)(b) requires that the defendant has the required *mens rea* for the ulterior offence when he or she commits it or attempts to commit it. He or she need not have the *mens rea* for the ulterior offence at the time of entry.

Conditional intent

Attorney General's Reference Nos. 1 and 2 of 1979 states that the defendant will still be guilty of burglary if he or she enters a building or part of a building with the intent to steal only if there is something worth stealing.

Evaluation

The meaning of 'entry'

The development of the interpretation of the word 'enters' in both s.9(1)(a) and s.9(1)(b) has substantially widened the definition in a way that makes it easier to convict for burglary. The case of *Collins* required the entry to be 'substantial and effective'. The judge in *Brown* decided that the entry need only be effective. In *Ryan*, the court decided that the entry did not need to be effective in that the defendant was able to carry out the ulterior offence.

The requirement of a trespass

Trespassing has always been an element of the civil law, requiring intentional, reckless or negligent entry into a building without the consent of the occupier (as defined in *Archbold*). Professor Smith argued that the *mens rea* for trespassing should not include civil words such as 'negligent'. Instead, it should use 'intention' or 'reckless' in a criminal sense. Professor Griew went further with his definition of the *mens rea* of a trespasser. He argued that the defendant personally must intend or at least see a risk that he or she is a trespasser, thus making the definition subjective. The Court of Appeal in *Collins* favoured Professor Griew's definition, meaning that 'trespasser' is defined as a criminal term rather than a civil term.

Ulterior offences

It is confusing for the average person/juror that burglary can be committed even when the defendant does not steal or even try to steal. Section 9(1)(a) requires the defendant only to intend to commit either theft, criminal damage or grievous bodily harm (these are known as the ulterior offences and are defined in s.9(2)).

The ulterior offences have been modernised slightly. Before the **Sexual Offences Act 2003**, the intention to commit rape was also an ulterior offence and would result in a conviction for burglary.

The definition of 'building'

The **Theft Act 1968** does not actually define 'building'. It does, however, give some examples of 'vehicles and vessels' in s.9(4). This means that the word 'building' also includes caravans and houseboats. Judges still use the common-law definition from *Stevens* v *Gourley* (1859). *B and S* v *Leathley* (1979) and *Norfolk Constabulary* v *Seeking and Gould* (1986) both rested on whether the courts considered trailers that were being used as storage containers to be buildings. The distinction was made by the courts that a container that has wheels attached is *not* a building, whereas a contained that has had its wheels removed *is* a building.

15 Robbery

Robbery is defined in the **Theft Act 1968**. According to s.8:

> A person is guilty of robbery if he steals, and immediately before or at the time of doing so, he uses force on any person or puts or seeks to put any person in fear of being subjected to force.

A Actus reus

Robbery is theft aggravated by the threat or use of force. Its *actus reus* therefore overlaps with that for theft (appropriation of property belonging to another), but has the additional requirement of force or threat of force on any person immediately before or at the time of stealing.

1 Theft (appropriation of property belonging to another)

In robbery, the appropriation does not have to be complete, as long as the defendant assumes one of the rights of the owner.

***Corcoran* v *Anderton* (1980)**
One of the defendants hit the victim across the back while the other pulled at her handbag. The victim screamed as the handbag fell to the ground and the defendants ran off empty handed. The defendants were found guilty of robbery. The appropriation occurred when the defendant grabbed the bag. It did not matter that the bag was then dropped, as he had assumed at least one of the rights of the owner when he grabbed it. The theft was complete and therefore the charge was one of robbery rather than attempted robbery.

2 Force or threat of force

The force does not need to be applied directly to the victim, and can instead be applied to the property.

***R* v *Clouden* (1987)**
The defendant wrenched a shopping bag from the victim's hand. The Court of Appeal held that the force applied to the property was sufficient to amount to robbery. What amounts to force should be left to the jury to decide.

The Criminal Law Revision Committee has criticised the decision in this case.

***R* v *Dawson and James* (1976)**
One of the defendants nudged the victim in the back so that he lost his balance. The other defendant took the victim's wallet. The amount of force used was sufficient to be classed as robbery. The word 'force' has been interpreted in the ordinary sense of the word. It does not require any violence.

2.1 On any person

The person upon whom the force is used or threatened does not have to be the same person who is stolen from. For example, someone can threaten a shop assistant and then steal from the owner of the shop.

2.2 Immediately before or at the time of stealing

The court has to decide how 'immediate' the threat must be before the stealing and at what point the theft is complete. One defendant can apply the force while the other defendant commits the theft. The theft can be seen as a continuing act.

***R* v *Hale* (1978)**
The defendants forced their way into the victim's house. One of the defendants went upstairs and stole a jewellery box while the other used force to tie up the victim. The Court of Appeal upheld their conviction for robbery, despite the fact that it was impossible to say whether the theft occurred at the same time as the force. The theft was a continuing act and therefore it was still happening when the victim was being tied up.

***R* v *Lockley* (1995)**
The decision of *Hale* was applied in this case. The defendants stole cans of beer from an off-licence and used force on the shopkeeper as they left the shop. The Court of Appeal upheld their conviction.

B *Mens rea*

The *mens rea* of robbery is the *mens rea* of theft (dishonesty and intention to permanently deprive), plus intentional or reckless application of force.

***R* v *Robinson* (1977)**
The victim owed the defendant money. The defendant used a knife to threaten the victim. The victim dropped a £5 note that the defendant took as part payment of the £7 he was owed. The Court of Appeal quashed his conviction for robbery, as the jury at his trial should have been allowed to consider whether he was not acting dishonestly due to the fact that he honestly believed he had a right in law to take the money.

This case illustrates that it is necessary first to prove theft before a charge of robbery can be considered.

C Evaluation

The current law on robbery affords three main criticisms relating to the:
- degree of force required
- lack of any distinction between different types of robbery
- large increase in the number of robberies being committed

Only 3% of reported robberies result in a conviction and the majority of robberies are committed using a threat of force rather than actual force.

1 *Degree of force required*

The degree of force required to turn a theft into a robbery is slight, yet the difference in punishment ranges from a maximum of 7 years' imprisonment for theft to life imprisonment for robbery.

See *R* v *Clouden* (1987) and *R* v *Dawson and James* (1976) on page 129.

2 No distinction between different types of robbery

Robbery is an indictable offence that must be tried at the Crown Court. Andrew Ashworth (2002) suggests that there should be two types of robbery: a lesser charge where the force is slight and a more serious charge where the force is greater. The less serious robberies could be tried at the Magistrates' Court and the serious robberies would continue to be tried at the Crown Court. This would save the courts valuable time and money.

3 Increase in robberies

There has been a massive increase in the number of robberies that are reported to the police. This is especially true of incidents involving street muggings for mobile phones. In 2002, Lord Woolf encouraged the use of prison sentences for such offences. However, due to the low conviction rates and the fact that most defendants aged under 18 get a community-based sentence for robbery, it is unlikely that there is much of a deterrent associated with such crimes.

Summary of Topic 15

Robbery is defined in the **Theft Act 1968**. According to s.8:

> A person is guilty of robbery if he steals, and immediately before or at the time of doing so, he uses force on any person or puts or seeks to put any person in fear of being subjected to force.

Actus reus

Robbery is theft aggravated by the threat or use of force. Its *actus reus* therefore overlaps with that for theft (appropriation of property belonging to another), but has the additional requirement of force or threat of force on any person immediately before or at the time of stealing.

Theft (appropriation of property belonging to another)

In robbery, the appropriation does not have to be complete, as long as the defendant assumes one of the rights of the owner (*Corcoran* v *Anderton*, 1980).

Force or threat of force

The force does not need to be applied directly to the victim, and can instead be applied to the property (*R* v *Clouden*, 1987 and *R* v *Dawson and James*, 1976).

On any person

The person upon whom the force is used or threatened does not have to be the same person who is stolen from.

Immediately before or at the time of stealing

The court has to decide how 'immediate' the threat must be before the stealing and at what point the theft is complete. One defendant can apply the force while the other defendant commits the theft. The theft can be seen as a continuing act (*R* v *Hale*, 1978 and *R* v *Lockley*, 1995).

Mens rea

The *mens rea* of robbery is the *mens rea* of theft (dishonesty — *R* v *Robinson* (1977) — and intention to permanently deprive), plus intentional or reckless application of force.

Evaluation

The current law on robbery affords three main criticisms relating to the:

- degree of force required
- lack of any distinction between different types of robbery
- large increase in the number of robberies being committed

Only 3% of reported robberies result in a conviction and the majority of robberies are committed using a threat of force rather than actual force.

OPIC 16 Making off without payment

Notice that 'making off' is defined in the Theft Act 1978 as opposed to the 1968 Act, which defines theft. This is an offence triable either way, with a maximum sentence of 2 years' imprisonment.

'Making off without payment' is defined in s.3 of the **Theft Act 1978**:

> A person who, knowing that payment on the spot for any goods supplied or services done is required or expected from him, dishonestly makes off without having paid as required or expected and with intent to avoid payment.

This offence is different from theft, as the defendant forms the *mens rea* after he or she has obtained ownership of the property.

A Actus reus

There are three parts to the *actus reus* for this offence:

- makes off
- without payment
- goods supplied or services done

1 Makes off

The actual spot that the defendant 'makes off' from is usually the place or point where payment is required.

***R* v *McDavitt* (1981)**
The defendant refused to pay for his meal in a restaurant. He made his way to the door but decided not to leave as the police had been called. The Crown Court decided that he had not made off, as he had not left the restaurant. It did not matter that he intended to leave without paying.

2 Without payment

The payment must be required or expected at the time that the defendant makes off. If the defendant makes an agreement that he or she will pay for the goods or services at a later date, the offence has not been committed.

***R* v *Vincent* (2001)**
The defendant stayed at two hotels for 5 weeks and ran up a bill totalling £1,300. He left the hotels after arranging with the managers to pay at a later date. The Court of Appeal quashed his conviction. He had not committed the *actus reus*, as payment was not expected when he left the hotels. It did not matter that he never intended to pay and had dishonestly made arrangements to pay later.

3 Goods supplied or services done

The most commonly used examples of 'goods supplied or services done' are when a person fills up his or her car with petrol and drives off without paying, or when someone has a meal in a restaurant and leaves without paying the bill.

It would not be an offence to make off without paying a drug dealer.

The goods and services must be ones where payment is legally enforceable. Section 3(3) states that there is no offence committed when the goods or services are against the law.

B Mens rea

There are three parts to the *mens rea* for this offence:
- dishonesty
- knowledge that payment is required
- intent to avoid payment

1 Dishonesty

The test for dishonesty for this offence is the same as that used for the offence of theft. The Court of Appeal established a two-stage test for dishonesty in *R* v *Ghosh* (1982). It combines both an objective and a subjective element. The jury has to answer the following questions:
- Has the defendant been dishonest by the ordinary standards of reasonable and honest people?
- If the answer is yes to the first question, the court should ask whether the defendant realised that he or she was dishonest by those standards. If the answer is yes to the second question, there is dishonesty.

2 Knowledge that payment is required

***Troughton* v *Metropolitan Police* (1987)**
Payment for taxi rides is usually expected at the end of the journey, but in this case the journey was never completed. The defendant asked the taxi driver to take him to Highbury but did not give an actual address. The taxi driver drove to Highbury in London but still could not ascertain the address, as the defendant was drunk. The taxi driver then drove to the police station where the defendant got out of the taxi and ran away. His conviction for making off was quashed by the Queen's Bench Divisional Court.

***R* v *Aziz* (1993)**
The facts of this case are similar to *Troughton*, except that the defendant had reached his destination but refused to pay. The taxi driver drove towards the police station, when the defendant forced him to stop the taxi and ran away. His conviction was upheld as he had completed his journey and payment for the service was expected.

3 Intent to avoid payment

The defendant must intend to avoid payment permanently. If the defendant claims that he or she was intending to pay at a later date, it is up to the jury to decide if it believes the defendant or not.

R v *Allen* (1985)

The defendant left his belongings at a hotel and departed without paying the bill. He telephoned the hotel and said that he would return a few days later and would leave his passport with them until he had enough money to pay. He was arrested when he returned to the hotel and convicted of making off. The House of Lords quashed his conviction; the jury at his trial should have been asked if it believed that he did intend to pay in the future.

Summary of Topic 16

'Making off without payment' is defined in s.3 of the **Theft Act 1978**:

> A person who, knowing that payment on the spot for any goods supplied or services done is required or expected from him, dishonestly makes off without having paid as required or expected and with intent to avoid payment.

Actus reus

Makes off

The actual spot that the defendant 'makes off' from is usually the place or point where payment is required (*R* v *McDavitt*, 1981).

Without payment

The payment must be required or expected at the time that the defendant makes off. If the defendant makes an agreement that he or she will pay for the goods or services at a later date, the offence has not been committed (*R* v *Vincent*, 2001).

Goods supplied or services done

The most commonly used examples of 'goods supplied or services done' are when a person fills up his or her car with petrol and drives off without paying, or when someone has a meal in a restaurant and leaves without paying the bill. The goods and services must be ones where payment is legally enforceable. Section 3(3) states that there is no offence committed when the goods or services are against the law.

Mens rea

Dishonesty

The same test is used as that for the offence of theft (*R* v *Ghosh*, 1982).

Knowledge that payment is required

See *Troughton* v *Metropolitan Police* (1987) c.f. *R* v *Aziz* (1993).

Intent to avoid payment

The defendant must intend to avoid payment permanently. If the defendant claims that he or she was intending to pay at a later date, it is up to the jury to decide if it believes the defendant or not (*R* v *Allen*, (1985).

TOPIC 17 Criminal damage

Criminal damage is defined in the **Criminal Damage Act 1971**. It may be aggravated if the defendant intends or is reckless as to whether life will be endangered. The crime of criminal damage also includes arson.

A Standard criminal damage

Criminal damage is defined in s.1(1) of the **Criminal Damage Act 1971**:

> A person who without lawful excuse destroys or damages any property belonging to another intending to destroy or damage or being reckless as to whether property is being destroyed or damaged commits an offence.

1 Actus reus

1.1 Destroys or damages

The amount of damage needs to be sufficient.

***A (a juvenile)* v *R* (1978)**
Spitting on a policeman's coat was not sufficient to constitute criminal damage as it could be easily wiped off.

The damage should affect the value or usefulness of the property.

***Morphitis* v *Salmon* (1990)**
A scratch to a scaffolding pole did not constitute criminal damage.

It is considered that damage has been caused when the property requires cleaning that has to be paid for.

The damage does not have to be permanent.

***Hardman* v *Chief Constable of Avon and Somerset Constabulary* (1986)**
The defendant drew a picture on the pavement with chalk. This was regarded as criminal damage as the council had to pay to have it cleaned off.

1.2 Property

'Property' is defined in s.10(1) of the **Criminal Damage Act 1971**:

> ...property of a tangible nature whether real or personal including money.

The definition of property for criminal damage is different to that for theft. It includes land (which theft does not), but it does not include intangible property such as shares (which is included in theft).

***R* v *Whiteley* (1991)**
The criminal damage does not have to be tangible, however the property that is damaged needs to be tangible. The defendant was convicted of criminal damage when he hacked into a computer and changed information stored on disks.

This situation would now be covered by s.3(1) of the **Computer Misuse Act 1990**, which makes it an offence to commit 'unauthorised modification of computer material'.

1.3 Belonging to another

'Belonging to another' is defined in s.10(2) of the **Criminal Damage Act 1971**:

> ...where the other has custody or control of it; or has a proprietary right or interest in it; or has charge of it.

This is similar to the crime of theft, yet the **Criminal Damage Act 1971** uses the words 'custody or control', whereas the **Theft Act 1968** uses the word 'possession'.

1.4 Without lawful excuse

'Without lawful excuse' is defined in s.5 of the **Criminal Damage Act 1971**:

> (a) If at the time of the act or acts alleged to constitute the offence he believed that the person or persons whom he believed to be entitled to consent to the destruction of or damage to the property in question had so consented, or would have consented to it if he or they had known of the destruction or damage and its circumstances: or
> (b) at the time of the act or acts alleged to constitute the offence he believed
> (i) that the property, right or interest was in immediate need of protection; and
> (ii) that the means of protection adopted or proposed to be adopted were or would be reasonable having regard to all the circumstances.

These defences apply to criminal damage, aggravated criminal damage and arson.

Sections 5(2)(a) and 5(2)(b) provide a statutory defence to criminal damage:

- Section 5(2)(a) covers the situation where the defendant believes that the owner would have consented to the damage.
- Section 5(2)(b) allows damage to occur when the defendant believes other property was in immediate need of protection.

***R* v *Denton* (1982)**
The defendant was not guilty of arson (discussed on page 139) when he set fire to his employer's mill, because he believed that the employer wanted him to do so in order to claim off the insurance (s.5(2)(a)).

Consent from God did not afford the defence in s.5(2)(a) when a vicar wrote a biblical quote on a pillar in the case of *Blake* v *DPP* (1993).

Section 5(3) provides that the defendant's 'belief' required in s.5(2)(a) and s.5(2)(b) is honestly held. It does not require the belief to be reasonable or justified, as long as it is honest.

***Jaggard* v *Dickinson* (1980)**
The defendant made a drunken mistake when she broke the victim's window. She thought that she was breaking the window at her boyfriend's house (something she thought he would consent to so that she could get in the house). Her defence was successful as she had an honest belief (regardless of the fact that it was not a reasonable belief).

1.5 Immediate protection

Section 5(2)(b)(i) requires the property to be in need of 'immediate protection' to allow the defence.

***R* v *Hill and Hall* (1988)**
The defendant feared that a nearby US naval base would come under nuclear attack and, therefore, her property would also be damaged. The defence was not allowed, as the threat from a nuclear attack was not 'immediate'.

The defences defined in s.5(2)(a) and s.5(2)(b) have always been regarded as subjective (based on what the defendant honestly believed). The courts have since added an objective element into s.5(2)(b). It is up to the jury/magistrates to decide if they believe that the defendant acted to prevent damage to property (not whether the defendants themselves thought they had acted to prevent damage to property). This was established in *R* v *Jones* (2004), where the defendants damaged a military base in the hope that it would prevent an attack on Iraq.

2 Mens rea

According to s.1(1) of the **Criminal Damage Act 1971**, the defendant must be either 'intending to destroy or damage or being reckless as to whether property is being destroyed or damaged'.

2.1 Intention

The defendant intended to cause damage or destruction by an act or omission.

***R* v *Smith* (1974)**

The defendant damaged fixtures that he had fitted in a flat he was renting. He was not guilty of criminal damage as he thought the fixtures belonged to him, even though legally they were the property of the landlord.

2.2 Recklessness

Before 2003, the test for recklessness was regarded as objective and was known as Caldwell objective recklessness (named after the case that established this rule). Since the case of *R* v *R and G* (2003), the test for recklessness is Cunningham subjective recklessness (a conscious taking of an unjustified risk).

***R* v *R and G* (2003)**

Two young boys threw lit newspaper into a bin that set fire to a shop, causing £1 million of damage. The House of Lords took the opportunity to change the test for reckless criminal damage from an objective test to a subjective test.

B Aggravated criminal damage

This offence has a maximum sentence of life imprisonment.

Aggravated criminal damage is defined in s.1(2) of the **Criminal Damage Act 1971**:

> A person who without lawful excuse destroys or damages any property, whether belonging to himself or another:
> (a) intending to destroy or damage any property or being reckless as to whether any property would be destroyed or damaged: and
> (b) intending by the destruction or damage to endanger life of another or being reckless as to whether the life of another would be thereby endangered shall be guilty of an offence.

1 Actus reus

This is similar to that for the crime of criminal damage, but it does allow for the property that is damaged to belong to the defendant.

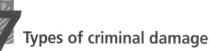

1.1 Endangering life

The offence does not require that actual lives are endangered, as long as the defendant *intends* to endanger life or is *reckless* as to whether life is endangered.

R v *Sangha* (1988)
The defendant set fire to furniture in his neighbour's flat. It did not matter that no lives were actually endangered because of the special design of the building, which prevented fire from spreading. The defendant was still convicted of aggravated criminal damage.

2 Mens rea

Professor Smith has criticised the fact that a crime that endangers life is contained in the property offence of criminal damage. He argued that it should be an offence against the person.

According to s.1(2)(a) and s.1(2)(b), the defendant must intend to damage or destroy property or be reckless, and intend life to be endangered or be reckless.

R v *Steer* (1988)
The defendant fired a gun at the victim through a window. The bullet missed the victim but hit the window, damaging it. The defendant was not guilty of aggravated criminal damage because it was not the criminal damage but the firing of the gun that had caused life to be endangered.

R v *Warwick* (1995)
This case differs from *R* v *Steer* (1988), as the Court of Appeal upheld the conviction of a defendant who threw a brick at a police car, which smashed the window and covered the policeman with glass, thus endangering his life.

C Arson

This offence has a maximum sentence of life imprisonment.

Arson is defined in s.1(3) of the **Criminal Damage Act 1971**:

> An offence committed under this section by destroying or damaging property by fire shall be charged as arson.

1 Actus reus

There must be some damage or destruction caused by fire. Singed material would be enough to constitute arson, but property blackened by smoke would not.

2 Mens rea

The defendant must either intend or be reckless that property will be damaged or destroyed by fire. There is also an offence of aggravated arson, where the defendant intends or is reckless that life may be endangered by fire.

The *mens rea* of arson can be formed after the fire has been started.

This case is also an example of an omission and contemporaneity.

R v *Miller* (1983)
The defendant accidentally set fire to a mattress when he fell asleep and dropped a lit cigarette. He formed the *mens rea* when he awoke and did nothing to extinguish the fire.

Summary of Topic 17

Standard Criminal damage

Criminal damage is defined in s.1(1) of the **Criminal Damage Act 1971**:

> A person who without lawful excuse destroys or damages any property belonging to another intending to destroy or damage or being reckless as to whether property is being destroyed or damaged commits an offence.

Actus reus

Destroys or damages

- The amount of 'damage' needs to be sufficient (*A (a juvenile)* v *R*, 1978).
- The 'damage' should affect the value or usefulness of the property (*Morphitis* v *Salmon*, 1990).
- It is regarded as 'damage' when the property requires cleaning that has to be paid for (*Hardman* v *Chief Constable of Avon and Somerset Constabulary*, 1986).

Property

- Section 10(1): 'property of a tangible nature whether real or personal including money'

The definition of property for criminal damage is different to that for theft. It includes land, but it does not include intangible property (*R* v *Whiteley*, 1991). Although the property that is damaged needs to be tangible, the criminal damage does not have to be tangible.

Belonging to another

- Section 10(2): 'where the other has custody or control of it; or has a proprietary right or interest in it; or has charge of it'.

This is similar to the crime of theft, yet the **Criminal Damage Act 1971** uses the words 'custody or control', whereas the **Theft Act 1968** uses the word 'possession'.

Without lawful excuse

Sections 5(2)(a) and 5(2)(b) provide a statutory defence to criminal damage:

- Section 5(2)(a) covers the situation where the defendant believes that the owner would have consented to the damage (*R* v *Denton*, 1982 and *Blake* v *DPP*, 1993).
- Section 5(2)(b) allows damage to occur when the defendant believes other property was in immediate need of protection (*R* v *Hill and Hall*, 1988).

Section 5(3) provides that the defendant's 'belief' required in sections 5(2)(a) and 5(2)(b) is honestly held. It does not require the belief to be reasonable, as long as it was honest (*Jaggard* v *Dickinson*, 1980).

Mens rea

According to s.1(1) of the **Criminal Damage Act 1971**, the defendant must either intend to destroy or damage property (*R* v *Smith*, 1974) or be reckless as to whether property is destroyed or damaged (*R* v *R and G*, 2003).

Aggravated criminal damage

Aggravated criminal damage is defined in s.1(2) of the **Criminal Damage Act 1971**:

> A person who without lawful excuse destroys or damages any property, whether belonging to himself or another,

> (a) intending to destroy or damage any property or being reckless as to whether any property would be destroyed or damaged: and
> (b) intending by the destruction or damage to endanger life of another or being reckless as to whether the life of another would be thereby endangered shall be guilty of an offence.

Actus reus

This is similar to the crime of criminal damage but does allow for the property that is damaged to belong to the defendant. It does not require that actual lives be endangered, as long as the defendant intends to endanger life or is reckless (*R* v *Sangha*, 1988).

Mens rea

According to sections 1(2)(a) and 1(2)(b), the defendant must intend to damage or destroy property or be reckless, and intend life to be endangered or be reckless (*R* v *Steer*, 1988 c.f. *R* v *Warwick*, 1995).

Arson

Arson is defined in s.1(3) of the **Criminal Damage Act 1971**:

> An offence committed under this section by destroying or damaging property by fire shall be charged as arson.

Actus reus

There must be some damage or destruction caused by fire. Singed material would be enough to constitute arson, but property blackened by smoke would not.

Mens rea

The defendant must either intend or be reckless that property will be damaged or destroyed by fire. There is also an offence of aggravated arson, where the defendant intends or is reckless that life may be endangered by fire.

The *mens rea* of arson can be formed after the fire has been started (*R* v *Miller*, 1983).

TOPIC 18 Deception

These crimes cover situations where the defendant receives property, services or an advantage by lying/being fraudulent.

A Obtaining property by deception

The offence of obtaining property by deception is described in s.15 of the **Theft Act 1968**:

> A person who by any deception dishonestly obtains property belonging to another with the intention of permanently depriving the other of it, shall on conviction on indictment be liable to imprisonment for a term not exceeding 10 years.

1 Actus reus

1.1 Obtaining

'Obtaining' is defined in s.15(2) of the **Theft Act 1968**:

> For the purposes of this section a person is to be treated as obtaining property if he obtains ownership, possession or control of it, and 'obtain' includes obtaining for another or enabling another to obtain or to retain.

This is similar to the concept of 'appropriation', as defined in the offence of theft. Since *R* v *Gomez* (1993), which established that theft could still occur even when the owner consents, the main difference between theft and obtaining property by deception is the need for deception.

The important case of *R* v *Preddy* (1996) led to the creation of the **Theft (Amendment) Act 1996**, which created a new crime of obtaining a money transfer by deception. This was because a money transfer could not be regarded as being 'obtained', whereas it could be seen as 'appropriation', which only requires assuming one of the rights of the owner. The other problem concerning this case was that the transfer could not be regarded as property belonging to another. Since the passing of the **Theft (Amendment) Act 1996**, such a situation is now regarded as a criminal offence.

1.2 Property

This is the same as for the offence of theft. However, it can include land, wild animals and plants.

'Property' is defined in s.4(1) of the **Theft Act 1968**:

> Property includes money and all other property, real or personal, including things in action and other intangible property.

1.3 Belonging to another

This is the same as for the offence of theft.

'Belonging to another' is defined in s.5(1) of the **Theft Act 1968**:

> Property shall be regarded as belonging to any person having possession or control over it, or having any proprietary right or interest.

1.4 By deception

'By deception' is defined in s.15(4) of the **Theft Act 1968**:

> For the purposes of this section 'deception' means any deception (whether deliberate or reckless) by words or conduct as to fact or as to law, including a deception as to the present intentions of the person using the deception or any other person.

1.4a Words or conduct

The victim must rely on the false statement or conduct.

***R* v *Laverty* (1970)**
The defendant changed the number plate on a car and then sold it on. His conduct could be seen as an implied representation that the number plates were on the correct car. The Court of Appeal eventually quashed the conviction, as it could not be proved that the deception had caused the buyer to pay for the car.

The 'words or conduct' must be the cause of the obtaining of property.

***DPP* v *Ray* (1974)**
The defendant had a meal in a restaurant, which he initially intended to pay for. His conduct was that of an ordinary customer. When he decided not to pay, he deceived the waiter by continuing to act as an ordinary honest customer. This caused the waiter to believe that he could leave the room, at which point the defendant ran off. The House of Lords upheld his conviction.

Using a credit card or chequebook that a person is not entitled to use is regarded as deception. It does not matter if the credit card or chequebook actually belongs to that person.

***Metropolitan Police Commissioner* v *Charles* (1977)**
The defendant was told not to write cheques for more that £30, as his bank account was overdrawn. He wrote 25 cheques for £30 each during an evening in a casino. He was charged with obtaining money by deception as he used his chequebook and cheque guarantee card as if he had the bank's authority to do so.

A person who accepts a credit card knowing that the defendant is not entitled to use it would be party to a fraud.

***R* v *Lambie* (1981)**
The defendant used her credit card, even though she knew she had gone over her credit limit. She was found guilty of obtaining money by deception following the decision in *Metropolitan Police Commissioner* v *Charles* (1977).

The deception must precede the obtaining.

***R* v *Coady* (1996)**
The defendant put petrol in his car and then told the petrol attendant that the company he worked for would pay for it. The Court of Appeal quashed his conviction because the petrol had already been obtained before he made the false statements (deception) to the petrol attendant.

2 Mens rea

2.1 Deliberate or reckless deception

Deliberate or reckless deception means that the defendant must commit the offence intentionally or recklessly. It does not matter if the defendant knows whether his statement or conduct is true or false.

2.2 Dishonesty

The Court of Appeal established a two-stage test for dishonesty in *R* v *Ghosh* (1982). It combines both an objective and a subjective element. The jury has to answer the following questions:

- Has the defendant been dishonest by the ordinary standards of reasonable and honest people?
- If the answer is yes to the first question, the court should ask whether the defendant realised that he or she was dishonest by those standards. If the answer is yes to the second question, there is dishonesty.

This is the same as for the offence of theft.

According to the **Theft Act 1968**, a defendant's willingness to pay does not necessarily mean that he or she was not dishonest. This is mentioned in s.2(2):

> Willingness to pay does not prevent a finding of dishonesty.

2.3 Intention to permanently deprive

This is the same as for the offence of theft.

'Intention to permanently deprive' is defined in s.6(1) of the **Theft Act 1968**:

> A person appropriating property belonging to another without meaning the other permanently to lose the thing itself is nevertheless to be regarded as having the intention of permanently depriving the other of it if his intention is to treat the thing as his own to dispose of regardless of the other's rights; and a borrowing or lending of it may amount to so treating it if, but only if, the borrowing or lending is for a period and in circumstances making it equivalent to an outright taking or disposal.

B Obtaining services by deception

This crime carries a maximum of 5 years' imprisonment.

'Obtaining services by deception' is defined in s.1 of the **Theft Act 1978**:

> A person who by any deception dishonestly obtains services from another shall be guilty of an offence.

1 Actus reus

1.1 Obtaining

This is the same as s.15 obtaining property by deception.

1.2 Services

'Services' is defined in s.1(2) of the **Theft Act 1978**:

> It is an obtaining of services where the other is induced to confer a benefit by doing some act, or causing or permitting some act to be done, on the understanding that the benefit has been or will be paid for.

Obtaining a free service is not an offence.

***R* v *Shortland* (1995)**
The defendant used a false identity to open bank accounts. The Court of Appeal quashed the conviction due to the requirement that the defendant must know that the service required payment. There was no evidence to suggest that the defendant knew this.

***R* v *Sofroniou* (2003)**
By using a false identity, the defendant deceived banks and credit card companies into giving him their services. The Court of Appeal upheld his conviction for the obtaining of banking and credit card services by deception. It believed that the defendant knew that such services required payment.

1.3 By deception

This is the same as s.15 obtaining property by deception.

2 Mens rea

The defendant must have the *mens rea* of deliberate or reckless deception and dishonesty. The *mens rea* is the same as for s.15 obtaining property by deception, but with one difference: it is not necessary for the defendant to have the intention to permanently deprive.

C Evasion of liability by deception

All three offences have a maximum sentence of 5 years' imprisonment.

The **Theft Act 1978** created three further offences known as evasion of liability by deception. Section 2(1) states that it is an offence if someone, by deception:

(a) dishonestly secures the remission of the whole or part of any existing liability to make a payment whether his own liability or another's
(b) with intent to make permanent default in whole or part of any existing liability to make a payment, or with intent to let another do so dishonestly induces the creditor to wait for payment (whether or not the due date for payment is deferred) or to forgo payment
(c) obtains by exemption from or abatement of liability to make payment

All three of these offences require:

- the *actus reus* of deception
- a legally enforceable liability to pay
- the creditor to be deceived
- the *mens rea* of intentional or reckless deception (s.2(1)(b) also requires intention to make permanent default)

1 *Remission (s.2(1)(a))*

Remission is where the defendant deceives the victim into believing that the defendant does not have to pay. Such situations are covered by s.2(1)(b) and (c).

Jackson could have equally been charged with s.2(1)(b).

***R* v *Jackson* (1983)**
The defendant used a stolen credit card to pay for petrol. This meant that Jackson had deceived the petrol station into looking for payment from the credit card company rather than from the defendant. He was convicted of s.2(1)(a).

2 Wait for or forgo (s.2(1)(b))

The defendant deceives the victim into waiting for the payment or waiving it completely.

***R* v *Holt and Lee* (1981)**
The defendants were in a restaurant when they were asked to pay for their meal. One of the defendants told the waiter that they had already paid one of the other waiting staff. This was untrue and they were convicted of s.2(1)(b).

3 Exemption from or abatement of liability (s.2(1)(c))

The defendant deceives the victim into letting him or her not pay in the future.

***R* v *Sibartie* (1983)**
The defendant deceived a ticket inspector that he had paid for the full train journey. He was charged with s.2(1)(c).

D Evaluation

1 Complexity

The definitions of deception are specific to each different situation. This means that the prosecution can have difficulty deciding which is the appropriate charge. To prevent this, the defendant may be charged with alternative offences, in the hope that one will be correct. For example, the defendant in *R* v *Vincent* (2001) was found not guilty of making off without payment (see Topic 16), yet he could have been found guilty of obtaining services by deception (s.1(1) of the **Theft Act 1978**).

All of these offences are technical, in the same way that the offence of theft is. This can lead to long and expensive trials, with defendants being found not guilty on a technicality.

2 Machines

Under the current law, it is impossible to deceive a machine. This means that there is a gap in the law relating to payment by credit card on the internet.

3 Obtaining property by deception

The Law Commission Report ('Fraud' 2002) criticises the cases of *Metropolitan Police Commissioner* v *Charles* (1977) and *R* v *Lambie* (1981) for the decision to convict regardless of whether the shop assistants who take stolen credit cards as payment would not do so if they knew the cards were stolen. The report states that, in the Law Commission's opinion, this does not constitute deception.

4 *Evasion of liability by deception*

These three offences were previously defined in s.16(2)(a) of the **Theft Act 1968**. The definition was problematic and unworkable so it was amended in the **Theft Act 1978** and is now contained in sections 2(1)(a), 2(1)(b) and 2(1)(c). However, the new definitions are still unsatisfactory. There are many overlaps between s.2(1)(a) and s.2(1)(b) in particular, with most cases falling under either definition, e.g. *R* v *Jackson* was charged with s.2(1)(a), whereas it could also have been s.2(1)(b).

5 *Overlap with other offences*

The deception offences could also be seen as theft cases. When a case could be deception or theft, the court in *R* v *Morris* (1983) said it is considered better to charge with deception first.

E Reform

The Law Commission wants to abolish all existing deception offences contained in the **Theft Acts 1968 and 1978** and to replace them with two offences of general fraud and obtaining services by deception.

1 *General fraud*

The Law Commission proposes:

> Any person who, with intent to make a gain or to cause a loss...dishonestly (1) makes a false representation, or (2) fails to disclose information to another person which (a) he...is under a legal duty to disclose, or (b) is of a kind which the other person trusts him...to disclose...or (3) abuses a position in which he...is expected to safeguard...the financial interests of another person...should be guilty of an offence of fraud.

2 *Obtaining services by deception*

The Law Commission proposes:

> Any person who by any dishonest act obtains services in respect of which payment is required, with intent to avoid payment, should be guilty of an offence of obtaining services dishonestly.

Summary of Topic 18

Obtaining property by deception

The offence of obtaining property by deception is described in s.15 of the **Theft Act 1968**:

> A person who by any deception dishonestly obtains property belonging to another with the intention of permanently depriving the other of it, shall on conviction on indictment be liable to imprisonment for a term not exceeding 10 years.

Actus reus

Obtaining

Section 15(2) of the **Theft Act 1968** states:

> For the purposes of this section a person is to be treated as obtaining property if he obtains ownership, possession or control of it, and 'obtain' includes obtaining for another or enabling another to obtain or to retain.

Property

This is the same as for the offence of theft.

Belonging to another

This is the same as for the offence of theft.

By deception

Section 15(4) of the **Theft Act 1968** states:

> For the purposes of this section 'deception' means any deception (whether deliberate or reckless) by words or conduct as to fact or as to law, including a deception as to the present intentions of the person using the deception or any other person.

Words or conduct

- The victim must rely on the false statement or conduct, e.g. *R* v *Laverty* (1970) and *DPP* v *Ray* (1974).
- Using a credit card or chequebook that a person is not entitled to use is regarded as deception. It does not matter if the credit card or chequebook actually belongs to that person, e.g. *Metropolitan Police Commissioner* v *Charles* (1977) and *R* v *Lambie* (1981).
- The deception must precede the obtaining, e.g. *R* v *Coady* (1996).

Mens rea

Deliberate or reckless deception

Deliberate or reckless deception means that the defendant must commit the offence intentionally or recklessly. It does not matter if the defendant knows whether his statement or conduct is true or false.

Dishonesty

This is the same as for the offence of theft.

Intention to permanently deprive

This is the same as for the offence of theft.

Obtaining services by deception

Section 1 of the **Theft Act 1978** states:

> A person who by any deception dishonestly obtains services from another shall be guilty of an offence.

Actus reus

Obtaining

This is the same as s.15 obtaining property by deception.

Services

Section 1(2) of the **Theft Act 1968** states:

> It is an obtaining of services where the other is induced to confer a benefit by doing some act, or causing or permitting some act to be done, on the understanding that the benefit has been or will be paid for.

Obtaining a free service is not an offence, e.g. *R* v *Shortland* (1995) and *R* v *Sofroniou* (2003).

By deception

This is the same as s.15 obtaining property by deception.

Mens rea

The defendant must have the *mens rea* of deliberate or reckless deception and dishonesty. The *mens rea* is the same as for s.15 obtaining property by deception, but with one difference: it is not necessary for the defendant to have the intention to permanently deprive.

Evasion of liability by deception

Section 2 of the **Theft Act 1978** created three further offences known as evasion of liability by deception. All three of these offences require:

- the *actus reus* of deception
- a legally enforceable liability to pay
- the creditor to be deceived
- the *mens rea* of intentional or reckless deception (s.2(1)(b) also requires intention to make permanent default)

Remission (s.2(1)(a))

Remission is where the defendant deceives the victim into believing that the defendant does not have to pay, e.g. *R* v *Jackson* (1983).

Wait for or forgo (s.2(1)(b))

The defendant deceives the victim into waiting for the payment or waiving it completely, e.g. *R* v *Holt and Lee* (1981).

Exemption from or abatement of liability (s.2(1)(c))

The defendant deceives the victim into letting him or her not pay in the future, e.g. *R* v *Sibartie* (1983).

Evaluation

Complexity

The definitions of deception are specific to each different situation. This means that the prosecution can have difficulty deciding which is the appropriate charge.

Machines

Under the current law, it is impossible to deceive a machine.

Obtaining property by deception

The Law Commission Report ('Fraud' 2002) criticises the cases of *Metropolitan Police Commissioner* v *Charles* (1977) and *R* v *Lambie* (1981).

Evasion of liability by deception

The definitions in the **Theft Act 1978** are unsatisfactory. There are many overlaps between s.2(1)(a) and s.2(1)(b).

Overlap with other offences

The deception offences could also be seen as theft cases.

Reform

The Law Commission wants to abolish all existing deception offences contained in the **Theft Acts 1968 and 1978** and to replace them with two offences of general fraud and obtaining services by deception.